PRAISE for Danielle LaPorte's *White Hot Truth*

"Danielle LaPorte's *White Hot Truth* comes straight from the messy, complicated world of **authentic life experience**. She is a force field of energy, wonder, humour, and love."

– **Eve Ensler**, author of *The Vagina Monologues* and *In The Body of the World*

"**Danielle LaPorte is a bright light in the modern priestesshood.** She keeps it spiritual, she keeps it real, she keeps it good."

– **Marianne Williamson**, NY Times bestselling author of *Tears to Triumph*

"Our souls are yearning for Danielle's liberating message—**that discernment is crucial to our true spiritual freedom**. She's as compassionate as she is fiery, and every contemporary seeker will see themselves in her hard won—and very timely—*White Hot Truth*."

– **Dr. Shefali Tsabary**, NY Times bestselling author of *The Awakened Family*

"Searing grace! **When Danielle LaPorte writes, there is nowhere to hide.** *White Hot Truth* is an incendiary device for the soul. Raw, honest, funny, wise, it's a portal to the part of you that's always wanted to see the light of day, but never quite knew how to find its way out. Read it. Live it. Breathe it. Be it."

– **Jonathan Fields**, author of *How to Live a Good Life*

"I devoured this book. The way Danielle questions our approach to self-actualization and reminds us what self-love truly looks and feels like is a revelation and a revolution. **Let this book be your guide to what you already know in your bones but may have forgotten as you've traversed the crowded spiritual growth industry.** Strip back the layers and remember the truth with a capital T."

– **Kate Northrup**, author of *Money: A Love Story*

"**This brave book is a substantial feast of truth singing and ecstatic wisdom** delivered by a fierce spirit called Danielle LaPorte. Your heart will leap in recognition and your soul will rise up mightily and do mighty things."

– **SARK**, co-author/artist of *Succulent Wild Love*

"A wonderfully engaging, deep-diving yet user-friendly tour of the promises and perils of 21st century spirituality. **Danielle casts a fiercely compassionate, psychologically savvy eye upon the ways in which we distract ourselves from what really matters.** Hers is a vividly alive, multi-colored invitation to embrace a life in which the personal, relational, and spiritual function as one."

– **Robert Augustus Masters**, PhD, author of *Spiritual Bypassing* and *To Be a Man*

"Danielle LaPorte never disappoints as this generation's go-to truth teller and visionary, always leading by being ahead of the curve. She intuits what is needed and provides it at the exact right moment. This holds true for her newest sizzling book-baby, *White Hot Truth*. Danielle is **empowering readers to trust their truth as she leads with her own vulnerability, wisdom, and wickedly good sense of humour.** A must-read for these tumultuous times!"

– **Terri Cole**, psychotherapist and creator of the *Real Love Revolution*

"I love real language. Communication without it is a diversion. I also recognize real insight, **it brings out your highest consciousness when you read it**...it's the "aha" that ignites you. *White Hot Truth* has all of this and far more...cover to cover."

– **Guru Singh**, Kundalini yoga & meditation master, author of *Buried Treasures*

"Danielle's voice is **medicine for self-help fatigue and ambition overdrive.** Her deep clarity and realness are a healing combination—and it's right on time for our culture."

– **Dr. Mark Hyman**, 10-time NY Times bestselling author

"In *White Hot Truth*, Danielle LaPorte graces us again with her creativity and courage. I consider Danielle one of the embodiments of prophetess in the modern age—she's a leader, a path-creator, and a vision keeper for hundreds of thousands of women in our time. Once again, in this book, **she raises the lantern of powerful words to help us see through the fog, and illumine a way forward.**"

– **Tara Mohr**, author of *Playing Big*

"Danielle LaPorte addresses the central question of our generation: Why is spiritual progress so confusing, full of nonsense, and plagued by false gurus? She's the fierce, daring, truth-slinging wingman we all need while on the authentic path of the soul. In her epic yet short book, I found the answers I've been seeking for decades."

– **Sara Gottfried**, NY Times bestselling author of *The Hormone Cure*

"Danielle lights the way in **reconnecting people to their true voice and authentic self**. Her words hold the power to validate, heal, and free the hearts and souls of womankind."

– **Anthony William**, #1 NY Times bestselling author of *Medical Medium Life-Changing Foods*

"When we share our stories and our struggles and the overcoming, we give others an opportunity to see themselves and to see that we all go through so much. Danielle does just this in *White Hot Truth*. She shares her journey with humour and wisdom allowing us to break through as she **explores the journey of an enlightened woman walking the path of the real life**. I inhaled *White Hot Truth* and bow to Danielle and the voice she brings to all."

– **Carrie-Anne Moss**, actress and founder of AnnapurnaLiving.com

"Danielle LaPorte is our soul's champion. She shines her white hot light on the radiance that lives in each of us."

– **Regena Thomashauer**, NY Times bestselling author of *Pussy*

"I've long said that Danielle LaPorte is one of the most beautiful writers alive today. *White Hot Truth* is Profound. Timely. Timeless. Danielle steps into a deeper leadership role as she blazes a SPIRIT path while also being **incredibly hip to the countless complexities of our very human experience/experiment**. Riveting!"

– **Linda Sivertsen**, bestselling author and host of *The Beautiful Writers Podcast*

"Danielle LaPorte's *White Hot Truth* is provocative, essential, devotional, sacred, profane, and necessary for all seekers...**an invitation for you to be brave and committed**. So get your courage on. Read it, be inspired by it, then read it again. Love lives in these pages."

– **Colette Baron-Reid**, author of *Uncharted* and creator of Oracle School

"Danielle LaPorte is a human hummingbird. Hummingbirds memorize thousands of flowers, but only go to the ones that truly nourish them. They are bright, intelligent creatures who cultivate the discernment to no longer be distracted by false images and pay special attention to the moments of illumination when their true nectar appears. *White Hot Truth* is **a must have how-to guide for efficiently and enjoyably traversing your daily life with less bullshit and more joy.** Danielle's words fly across the page sharing timeless eternal wisdom by making it accessible in a modern relatable context."

– **Rochelle Schieck**, author of *Qoya* and creator of www.Qoya.love

"**Poetic, visionary, and downright hysterical**, *White Hot Truth* reminds us that spirituality isn't about having the courage to just be real—it is to be the hot mess and the holy soul that we are."

– **Meggan Watterson**, author of *How to Love Yourself (and Sometimes Other People)*

"This is a book to be lived. Savour it. Delight in it. **Weep and laugh and belly your way through it. This is a gospel for our times.** A laser beam of truth that will "comfort the afflicted and afflict the comfortable." *White Hot Truth* is, ultimately, a love song. To our divinely human selves. To our beautiful, fractured world."

– **Hiro Boga**, creator of *Become Your Own Business Adviser*

"I love the tenderness with which Danielle sees the whole. Beautiful and funny and wry. This feels mature, wise-woman, and integrated. ***White Hot Truth* gives us permission to be ourselves when we are so caught up in being what we think we should be.** This book is a gift."

– **Lianne Raymond**, Master Coach

"Every paragraph of this book is a truthbomb. Danielle's way of naming what you feel in your bones but haven't yet identified is the gift of *White Hot Truth*. It's validating, it's wise, and—if you're ready—this is a **majorly liberating approach to becoming your best self**."

– **Eric Handler**, founder of PositivelyPostive.com

WHITE HOT TRUTH

White Hot Truth

**Clarity for keeping it real on your spiritual path—
from one seeker to another.**

Danielle LaPorte

=VIRTU∅NICA=
p u b l i s h i n g

WHITE HOT TRUTH Copyright © 2017 VIRTUONICA

Danielle LaPorte, Inc, Vancouver, Canada. All rights reserved.

Hardcover: ISBN 978-0-9976514-0-9

e-book: ISBN 978-0-9976514-5-4

audiobook: ISBN 978-0-9976514-6-1

Distributed in the US and Canada by Ingram Publisher Services, Inc.,
and in Australia by Phoenix Distribution.

Library of Congress Cataloguing-In-Publication Data is available on request.

Author's note: Out of respect, some names and identifying characteristics
in this work have been changed.

Content editor: Jennifer Gandin Le

Proofreading and indexing: StephenUllstrom.com

Proofreading: Kaitlyn Till

Cover and interior design: LaurieMillotte.com

Author photograph: CatherineJust.com

Interior typeface: Calluna by Exljbris, and Helvetica Neue by Linotype

Playlist on repeat: Yo-Yo Ma, Bach Cello Suite No. 1 in G Major

Printed in China by Spectrum Print Group

≡VIRTUØNICA≡
p u b l i s h i n g

An imprint of Danielle LaPorte, Inc.

DanielleLaPorte.com

@daniellelaporte ⊙ ⅄ f ℗ | **#whitehottruth**

#234-2055 Commercial Drive, Vancouver BC, V5N 0C7

MEDIA + SPEAKING: please contact media@daniellelaporte.com

SALES: for discounts and bulk purchases, please contact sales@daniellelaporte.com

ALL INQUIRIES: support@daniellelaporte.com

For my Girlfriends
past, present, future, and forever;
without whom I'd be the very unpleasant kind of crazy
and bankrupted by therapy bills.

You keep me close to everything that matters most.

I have been a seeker and still am
but I stopped asking the books and the stars.
I started listening to the teaching of my soul.
– Rumi

you think
you need
an architect,
but you
are already
a temple.

1

THE CHURCH OF SELF-IMPROVEMENT
When worship feels like work

Dearly beloved,
We are gathered here today 2 get through
this thing called life.
– Prince

"THREE SHRINKS WALK into a bar: a Buddhist, an agnostic, and a Catholic..."

This isn't a joke, it's my talk therapy history. I've had a life coach, a creativity coach, a speaking coach, an intuitive-business coach. I've had astrology readings with both western and eastern (those are called "Vedic") astrologers—because, you know, it's always good to have a backup astrologer in case you don't like what the first one predicts. I've communicated with the goddess Pele, and talked with my Spirit Guides and the Archangel Metatron. I've communed with my inner child, my future self, and the devas of my website. I've cleared dozens of past lives, dissolved some ancestral vows, and examined the fine print of my Soul contracts.

I've tried hypnotherapy to resolve my karma (turns out that I can't be put under the spell, so I might be stuck with the karma). I've suffered through wellness workshops led by chain-smoking megalomaniacs who treated their staff like morons. I've fire-walked barefoot down a twenty-foot bed of hot coals—without getting burned. I've chanted prayers in infrared saunas, then gotten rid of my microwave. I've taught myself the art of planning for synchronicity.

On the way to my first meeting at the White House, I tucked crystals into my bra for protection—they weren't detected by security because *that's* how magical amethysts can be. I've dropped mushrooms but refused painkillers. I've popped blue-green algae to pull all-nighters, brewed kombucha for my cha-cha. I have meditated while having a coffee colonic (and let me tell you, if you can meditate with a tube up your ass, you are definitely headed toward enlightenment). I've read channeling transcripts on how to find my Soulmate—for which I blame at least two breakups and a few missed opportunities to get laid by good men. If I'd been less fixated on the perfect twin flame, I might have been more easy...going. I temporarily broke up with the New Age to date New Physics. *Everything happens for a reason.*

Being on stage a lot as a "motivational speaker," I was sermonizing about healthy boundaries and self-Love being a divine responsibility. Most people seemed to think, *Well,* she *doesn't suffer fools.* But behind the scenes I was suffering some serious foolishness. I took a lot of crap from lovers and other collaborators because I thought tolerance was the "spiritual" course of action, or non-action as was the case. I practiced being less attached to my wants and more attached to my needs—but it was really hard to tell the difference. I chose Freddie Mercury as my Spirit Animal. He helped. *The show must go on.*

I have been the humble and awestruck recipient of full-on healing miracles. A medicine man from New Mexico pulled a deep pain from my psyche that I'd felt for years but could not name. As that ceremony was coming to a close, he waved an eagle feather over my head and said, "Only forward now, only forward." After a motorbike accident in Bali, I visited a local healer who pressed on my pain points. I bellowed in agony. He chanted, blew on my knees and ankles, and applied pressure again to the same places—and the pain was gone. Gifted girlfriends have laid their hands on me after my great losses. Their Love triggered somatic release and the deepest kind of relief—and the laughs that only women who've been there can laugh. And so many of us have been there.

I've been duped and harassed by a so-called energy healer, used for my Shakti, my cash, and my connections. In hindsight, that was a profound and absolutely essential initiation into my fuller capacities. I used to believe that the Light would win over the dark. Now I am radiant proof.

I have knelt at the feet of a Tibetan Buddhist lama and asked earnestly,

"Will you teach me about the heart of the matter?"

I have sat in lotus position watching my in-breath and my out-breath. I've consciously inhaled the suffering of tsunami survivors and breathed out comfort and rebuilding. I have learned about suppressed histories and the deepest possible feminism from the Gospel of Mary Magdalene. My perceptions of a score-keeping God were dissolving. As I've worked through my contentious relationship with meditation, very particular images of Light showed up for me that I would later find mirrored in science texts and sacred art.

I was getting closer to my Truth.

But first I had to see that somewhere between the yoga classes, support calls with a shaman, and guided visualizations, my spiritual path had become another to-do list, next to which scrolled an equally long list of life and career must-dos: crafting organic baby food and handmade birthday cards, achieving Inbox Zero, making my first million, and doing my part to save the planet from global warming.

I was a bit out of breath (both the in- and out-breaths) when I realized that I was at a jarring juncture: the conflict between **sincere spiritual aspiration** and **the compulsion to improve**.

I was tired. And still devoted to knowing more—always more. But mostly, tired.

Questioning the quest

One night, I was meditating in the bathtub. I had begun my day already feeling a bit "behind" because I'd skipped my sitting practice to sleep a few extra minutes before I woke my kid for school. I was learning to work with mantras, specifically for clearing obstacles. *Om Gam Ganapatayei Namaha.* So in the kitchen that morning, I'd cranked my mantra playlist (doesn't everyone have a Morning Mantra playlist?) while I scrambled some eggs for my little dude. No breakfast for me; I was on a juice cleanse. *Mom, that music is creepy. Can you put on some Bruno Mars?* Eat yer eggs.

Once my boy was off to school, I had an early therapy session on the phone. Next, a meeting with my business lawyer, followed by an interview with a magazine editor who wanted me to give their readers five easy tips for immediate enlightenment. ("Like, 'quickies' that everybody can do," they said with a straight face.) In between all of this I texted my besties about the rad insights I gleaned from my therapy session:

Me: Great shrink sesh. I said to him: I took the crumbs when they came. Tried to make a cake outta them. Shrink said: crumbs keep you starving, Danielle, not fed. Bam!
Chela: Fucking crumbs.
Me: STARVING.
Chela: Drop the mic!
Me: Makes me hungry.
Chela: Me too.

Back to my bathtub...

The day ends, and I'm soaking in my hot bath concoction of lavender oil (twelve drops), Himalayan pink salt (three cups, or Epsom salts will do), and apple cider vinegar (one cup). It's a classic brew to dispel and cleanse negative energy. I was reflecting on forgiveness, I was breathing with Light, and I was begging my angels and any other on-duty deity to help lift my pain from me, specifically the anguish of my divorce. *Please, take it from me, I'm so tired of it coming around again and again. I'll do whatever I need to do.*

I cried a good, heaving, sober of a cry. You know the kind. You go so guttural that once the pain is heaved out you're at the bottom of the bowl of your being. It's a sacred emptiness and... Hey, look! What's waiting there for you? It's your joy. All patient and steady, joy smiles and nods to you, "Good job. You got through it." It was one of those cries.

As I got out of the bath, the steam rising off my skin, I recounted all that I'd done that day, that week—hell, all that I'd been doing for two *decades* to keep my Soul in shape. I thought about what was written in my day planner: *Pick up protein powder. Book cabin for writing retreat.* There were more energy work appointments and yoga classes scheduled in. (I wrote smiley faces next to the days where I actually made it to yoga class.)

And then I looked at myself in the bathroom mirror. Naked, still, and silent. I leaned forward and my eyes asked:

"But do you feel free?"

Because freedom was, and is, the whole point. Countless teachers of mysticism throughout time concur that the reason for spiritual endeavouring is liberation and only liberation. Liberation from fear, from restrictive ideologies, from illusion, from suffering. Liberation from the anxiety of not being one's true self.

Free.

Are you feeling it?

Is everything you're doing to be well and liberated really helping you to be well and liberated? Because if liberation is a chore, then you aren't really free, are you?

> You can't seek approval on your way to sovereignty.
> Freedom is not something you need to earn.
> Joy does not come from a checklist.

I've had to fight for my joy. I've also loved and laughed and created my way to it. But it's fair to say that crushing the obstacles, torching the illusions, fielding the attacks, going down with the grief—it's been some strenuous work.

I think of the places that I made myself go to become intimate with the dualities of Love and expediency, Light and darkness, confusion and clarity. I got through those portals the scrappy, human way, the way mortals discover their connection to the cosmos: laughing really hard on the phone with girlfriends, and weeping alone on the kitchen floor. I did it with a home birth. Divorce. Building a career, word by word. Leaving it all on stage. Begging psychics for answers and pressing gurus for practicalities. Praying daily for the Light, to the Light, with the Light.

At this point in my life, I am the joy that I fought for.

Now that I'm here, very directly facing my Soul, I wonder if all that "hard self-help work" was a really messed up way to go about finding illumination? Could I have just accepted myself much sooner and saved a lot of money on therapy? Maybe. But probably not. Truth is a journey.

You have to Love yourself into fullness.

The valley of inquiry

*People will think they are good. They are simply suffering, because
the more "good" you think you are, the more nobody is okay for
you. If you're too good, no life can happen. It's not your goodness
that will liberate you... It's the joyfulness of your own nature.*

- Sadhguru

Underneath so much of our self-helping can be a lot of self-loathing.
We create new obsessions to replace our old addictions. Of course a
green smoothie is an immensely more nutritious choice than a soda
pop. Exercise and meditation have far more enjoyable side effects than
antidepressants. Practicing lovingkindness is perpetually awesome. But
often, certainly more than we admit to ourselves, we're stuck in a self-help
Groundhog Day. "I'm not good enough yet, but I'll get better. I'm getting
better at bettering myself. Am I better yet?" And repeat.

We're doing so many good and balanced things to grow and develop
ourselves—but maybe we're trying to get better for some unhealthy
reasons.

What's behind the compulsive drive to improve? Criticism. Trust me, I
know; I'm a highly self-critical self-improvement author. It's the criticism
that you absorb from how you were raised, as unintentional the harm of
your family's commentary may have been. It's the trauma carried over
from that lifetime when you were burned at the stake for being inquis-
itive. It's the old patriarchy still playing on your self-esteem. It seeps in
from every photoshopped image telling you that you should be thinner,
curvier (but only in the right places), whiter, browner, perfectly coiffed,
and perpetually positive as you balance your workout time, your thriving
career, and feed your well-behaved children non-genetically modified
food—and if you're not making time for all of those things, well, you must
not want it badly enough. Maybe what you need is another workshop on
finding your passion.

Lots of *believed* criticism makes for lots of effort to improve. Endless
effort. Relentless effort. Ruthless effort.

What happens when all of the life balance hacks don't yield our desired results? (You know that life balance is a total myth, right? It's the biggest self-help sham ever.) Or when we do get what we set out to achieve but we feel kind of empty when we get it? Well, then we just criticize ourselves even more harshly.

Spiritual passion can be punishing when it comes from the hollowness of our psyche rather than the fullness of our Spirit. Between striving and fullness there's a valley, and it's full of delicious questions. The more questions we ask, the more nourishment we bring to our lives—and each other.

Buddhists call the cycle of "wandering through life and death" *samsara*. The operative word here is "wandering," as in: we're ambling from lifetime to lifetime, sweating the small stuff, and not really seeing the bigger picture. The name of the evolution game is to wake up and get off the wheel of suffering—*samsara*—and onto the ground of full presence, which in turn creates inner peace. According to the Buddha's teachings, we exit the crazy ride when we stop craving for things to be different than they are. When we drop the illusions of separation and imperfection, we can enjoy the valley we find ourselves in.

Can you imagine *not* craving to be different than you are right now?

Take a breath.

For just a moment...can you stop craving to be any different than you are right now?

Because here's the sacred paradox: transformation begins with the radical acceptance of what is.

Pleasant distractions

The problem is that the desire to change is fundamentally a form of aggression toward yourself. The other problem is that our hang-ups, unfortunately or fortunately, contain our wealth. Our neurosis and our wisdom are made out of the same material. If you throw out your neurosis, you also throw out your wisdom.

– Pema Chödrön

I started to unpack what Love and spiritual commitment really meant to me, dismantling my assumptions, taking nothing for granted. I looked at every kind of relationship I was having: where I was generous, where I withheld, when I accepted things, and when I yelled. It took me a long time to notice that there were some holes in my boundaries. Big ones.

I also noticed that a lot of the women around me, who were reading the same books and listening to tele-summits on "Infinite Goddess Power & Unconditional Harmonious Love for an Unfolding Universe in Times of Change for the Modern Woman," were knocking themselves OUT to do the "right" spiritual thing—to be more loving, more flexible, more socially responsible, more forgiving, more giving. Powerful potential there—right? But there was a noticeable difference between the tolerance and latitude that they afforded others (way too much), and the forgiveness and compassion that they gave themselves (way too little). They were taking too much shit.

"We're going to try conscious uncoupling. I just downloaded the audios on it," a friend told me about herself and her soon-to-be ex-husband. I had to chime in. "Except that you're leaving him because he's so totally *unconscious*," I said. "What you need is a conscious lawyer."

For some women on "The Path," serious rage and sorrow was buried beneath the guided imagery and platitudes about pain.

Getting "spiritual" was delaying getting real.

Psychologist John Welwood coined a fabulous term: **spiritual bypassing**. He defines it as: "The use of spiritual practices and beliefs to avoid dealing with our painful feelings, unresolved wounds, and developmental needs." Brilliant, right? And the equally brilliant psychologist, Robert Augustus Masters (you should just read every book he's ever written), sums up the behaviours of spiritual bypassing as such:

"...exaggerated detachment, emotional numbing and repression, over-emphasis on the positive, anger-phobia, blind or overly tolerant compassion, weak or too porous boundaries, lopsided development, debilitating judgment about one's negative or shadow side, devaluation of the personal relative to the spiritual, and delusions of having arrived at a higher level of being."

Anyone? Ya, I thought so. Me too.

In short: all the woo is keeping us from dealing with our poo.

Instead of medicating with Marlboros and martinis, we might be doing it with metaphysics and macrobiotics. And unlike boozing it up to drown our pain, the side effects of neurotic psychoanalyzing or forced flexibility are difficult to spot. We don't end up in rehab from too much meditation or therapy—we just end up in more workshops. Think of that friend you have who has a not-so-loving relationship with her body, but because she eats "health foods" and talks a good "body positive" talk about just wanting to be strong, we cheer her on. But really, she's got self-destructive motivations and a mild eating disorder disguised as a holistic wellness routine. On the surface, positivity and wellness goalkeeping present so nicely that it can be hard to see when healthy actions are hooked to unhealthy ambitions.

Like too much of anything, spiritual bypassing can numb us out from our Truth—which is where the healing answers wait to be found.

Growing upward

Of course, not all seeking is distraction. Not everyone who's focused on Light is avoiding their dark side. For so very many of us, the devotion is pure-hearted and Soul-motivated. We're not running from or bypassing anything. We're using our spirituality to deal directly with every part of our lives—the painful parts, the blissful goodness, and the mystery of everything in between. We're dancing with the Divine because it turns us on to Life. So hot.

I've had some doozers of misjudgment and naïveté—total self-help escapades. Even so, I don't feel like one minute or dollar was wasted. (Except for that Ouija board phase in my early twenties. That was dumb. And that aura spray that was supposed to dispel negative energy. Rip-off.) Bad choices are how we learn to be discerning. We're experimenting, we're living into our Truth, we're *growing upward*. We're seeing if Yahweh's Ten Commandments or Buddha's Eightfold Path add up to anything useful for our morality. We're sampling some Hinduism; we're Pagan-curious. We're spiritually promiscuous or totally buttoned-up until just the right type of Truth shows up and we declare our Love and commitment to it.

But in the meantime, we test and exploit ourselves. Profusely. Not because we're weak or defective, but because that's what students of life do—they sign up to learn.

We give our power away—then we learn how undeniably powerful we are when we wrest it back. It's not an indeterminate failing that lesser-evolved people go through. **Power retrieval is an initiation for the brave hearts.**

If we lived in traditionally tribal environments, we might be put through a series of esoteric initiations to build our internal strength. But instead, for most of us, our initiations tend to come less formally and with less ritual. Life might give us a series of domineering bosses to teach us how to sense and slay deception—we learn how to see in the dark. We get a cancer diagnosis that spurs us to reach into multiple dimensions and modalities to heal the disease—we become alchemists. A child comes into our life with "special needs" and we turn on our latent telepathy. Our initiations may look more haphazard or pedestrian, but they are as divinely orchestrated and effectual as any rite of passage taken by an ordained monk or medicine woman.

Futility or utility?

Part of being a grown-up (a relative term) is knowing what's good for you. As we experiment with ideas, programs, and substances, we're fine-tuning our "what works" detectors. Gestalt therapy rocked your world for a few years, but now you're just so done talking about it. Bible study, hot yoga, flower essences, Rasta, shamanic drum journeying. Some explorations turn into lifelong practices, others we naturally outgrow, and sometimes—especially if we've been forcing our interest just to be cool—we wake up and wonder, *What was I thinking?*

I was sitting in a weekend Buddhist retreat at a theology school. A few yoga mats to the left of me sat a dude wearing purple drop-crotch cotton pants, and, of course, a tie-dye t-shirt and moccasins. He was in the throes of an intellectual wank-fest with the lama in charge about why the sky is blue. Not scientifically why the sky is blue, but why, as humans, we all "agree" to collectively perceive that the sky is blue. The basic gist: our deep consciousness resonates with the moving molecules of the sensory world and... I don't even come close to caring about intellectual abstractions. Like, I *so* don't care. Becaaause...

Because that particular weekend I was thinking, *I'm having a really shitty season and this information is not going to help me at all. Can we please talk about how I explain pornography to my kid in the context of Buddhist right action? And how do I transcend my ego as my public profile rises? And more to the point of my currently very raw heart, can we please talk about the karma of revenge that seems, you know, justified? Because my ex just accidentally sent me a very special text that was intended for his new girlfriend, and I'm thinking of bashing in his headlights on my way home tonight. But hey, go ahead and blather on about the sky being blue. I'm sure it's applicable for somebody with*

no worries or cares in the sentient world, or someone in this room...wearing
purple drop-crotch cotton pants and moccasins.

Not useful. Not useful at all.

I need a Truth I can work with. I want a spirituality that I can apply
to my everyday, ambitious, very private, somewhat public, sweet, little,
big, messy, gorgeous, desirous, meaningful, normal existence. I need a
"presence" that takes my entire life into consideration.

The hustle

Around that same time, I was starting to get the drift that, *heyyyy* not
all spiritual teachers were walkin' their meta-talk. I had dinner with an
ordained monk to discuss a global meditation campaign, and he was so
rude to the waiter that I left a fifty percent tip as an apology. I dragged a
friend to a lecture on "Transcending the Ego"—a night with a very popular
American guru-type guy. It was a only few weeks after the 9-11 terrorist
attacks in the U.S. and one audience member, after standing in the long
queue for questions, asked the expert how to deal with the trauma from
recent events. Monsieur No Ego, in his designer loafers, scoffed at him
from the stage. "I've come to talk about the ego, not events in the media."
Ohhhkaaay. The discomfort in the room was supersized. The man who
asked the question stuttered, "Well, I thought it was relevant," and then
slunk back to his seat. My friend and I looked at each other, aghast. I did
my best *WTF was THAT?!* face and then she mouthed to me, "What an
asshole." Naturally, that triggered an illegal giggle fit, and we had to do
the walk of shame out of the ballroom, giggling all the way.

Because I was working as a publicist in the personal-growth scene, I
heard my fair share of stories about naughty commune leaders and cranky
Kirtan singers, and authors with bestselling relationship advice books who
were embroiled in bitter divorces. Culturally, we're not as surprised when
a politician is busted for having extramarital affairs. But when you find
out that the wispy angel-channeler guy is having orgies, it's a little more

jarring—and a lot more entertaining. (New Age gossip is *the best*.) I think back on my gullibility of those days with fondness. Imagine: I thought that because their workshops were sold out, or because they'd studied in India, that the experts' motives matched their messages. It turns out that if you've got a good publicist, you can sell almost anything.

Dirty, messy, spiritual

> We want a path that would not be opposed to our life, a life
> that would not be opposed to our path. We want to attain
> a plentitude without denying life's marvelous effervescence;
> we want a light and moving joy that would bring us to a
> larger, more all encompassing experience of reality.
>
> – Daniel Odier, *Desire: The Tantric Path to Awakening*

My New Year's resolution a few years back was to be way mo' bad. My version of the "good" kind of bad. Smoke more. Drink more. Eat more red meat—really rare. I was willing to sleep around more, but it turns out that I'm too focused for that. What really turned me on was the idea of deleting everything in my inbox. Nasty girl hittin' DELETE! Clearly, nasty is a relative term.

I started coming across spiritual characters who had stepped out of bounds in life-affirming ways. Thomas Merton, a much-respected American Trappist monk, fell in love with a nurse who was tending to him. "I am humbled and confused by my weakness, my vulnerability, my passion," he wrote of their connection. After ending the relationship, he recommitted himself to his vows. I read about nuns who left the convent for romantic love. I was in my twelfth year of vegetarianism when I heard that the Dalai Lama, a lifelong vegetarian, had started eating beef at his doctor's insistence. Made me want a cheeseburger. A good friend of mine was on a retreat with a Zen roshi who had just given a genius teaching on the purity of the mind when she caught him smoking behind the temple during the break. Unfazed, he shrugged, took another drag, and said to her, "You can't take any of it too seriously," and exhaled a waft of smoke. Now there's a workshop takeaway.

> I was longing for another way to aspire, a fuller way to worship. I wanted to consume life, consciously but guilt-free. I wanted to express myself, considerately but without hesitation. I wanted a purity of Soul that wasn't puritanical. I wanted an intensity of intention, to go deep, and, at the same time, lighten up.

Sound + vision

I'm in the make-your-life-better industry. And it is an *industry*. My business engine is fuelled by my many "lists" of subscribers and online followers. My social media feeds are a steady stream of #Truthbombs and how-tos. And every once in awhile, I tell ya, I get so sick of hearing myself telling everyone else what to do.

So many books and blogs and supplements. So many opinions about how to up your mojo and sanctify your psyche. And I wonder if I've become jaded from seeing all the motivational fluff that infiltrates over Wi-Fi, while some of the truly masterful spiritual teachers of our time can't get book publishing deals because they don't have enough "likes" on Facebook. The self-help space has become another form of entertainment and, in too many cases, the loudest voices are the ones being listened to. So many consumers are mistaking volume for wisdom.

And...loud cheerleading isn't entirely a bad thing. Even if it's shallow, it's an expression of encouragement, and it can bring Light to a lot of wanderers. It's a step toward looking for more meaning.

We are making our way. We're figuring it out. We're harnessing the power of the Information Age because we want more for our lives. And it's bound to get weird and inspiring all at the same time. There are no straight lines to wisdom. If you think you've got a helpful message of your own to share, then get yourself a blog or claim five minutes at the next staff meeting and *preach*. Because your Truth may be the Light that lifts someone up that day. We need your voice. We need to hear the ideas that spring from your longing and your confidence.

You know that humanity and the ecosystem are in trouble. We're choking our lives and the Earth with our thoughtless consumption. The bees are dying. The starfish are melting. Increasingly, it's unsafe to drink our own water. We're selling humans to other humans, raping and being raped. We're turning children into killers. So many of us are numbed out, gluttonous, and greedy.

We are suffering. We are feeling the hunger pains for Truth, Light, and Faith.

We are learning to live for what really matters—both out of necessity and our innate impulse to evolve. We are waking up to deeper knowledge and extraordinary science. We're cleaning up our cities and opening up more borders than are being closed down. We're changing laws and policies to accommodate more expressions of Love. We're turning garbage into fuel and working to make social solutions profitable—financially and spiritually. We are mass-communicating with each other. We're creating and consuming copious amounts of inspirational and fact-based media about our greater potential. Steadily, we are listening more to the intelligence of our hearts—and acting on that wisdom. And that's what spirituality is—an expression of Love.

After a lifetime of seeking illumination, I'm not just gambling on this "spiritual thing" paying off. I'm totally in. I lust for Light. I'm here to serve, and I'll probably keep coming back to do just that. I still talk to angels every day. I guzzle turmeric tonic. I sweat my prayers. I have an energy worker on my advisory board, and I never launch a project during Mercury Retrograde. Not ever.

Some of us will live according to our Spirit Guides, or the Kabbalah, or ecstatic poetry. Some of us will go to spin class, study scripture, drink green juice, make love, make millions, marathon, mother, dance, or fire-breathe our way to higher Love.

Our fulfillment stems from our motives. It's not *how* we seek spiritual growth, it's *why* we seek it.

May you seek to know the vastness of your Light.

thank the
lies
for showing
you the
truth

2
THE REALLY BIG LIES
The falsities we (inevitably, and
necessarily) fall for on our way to Truth

seeker of truth

follow no path
all paths lead where

truth is here
– e. e. cummings

COMING OF AGE in the New Age gave me *a lot* of great material to work with in therapy. With years of chronic self-improvement behind me, I had puh-lenty of issues to unpack—past lifetimes of issues (as if this current lifetime wasn't enough), multidimensional issues, local issues, and global issues.

I read my first occult book when I was thirteen. Being a Catholic schoolgirl, this was thrilling and illicit material. (Really, what...schoolgirl?) A friend's mother passed some books on to me. She had the most beautiful boofy hair with ash-blonde highlights, and her beige lipstick went perfectly with her ivory power suits. She seemed like she'd just walked off the set of a made-for-TV movie. She had a special "healing" lamp in her bedroom with various coloured bulbs, one for each chakra. Their family was always talking about "guides" and "aura readings." With her glamorous style and all that esoteric conversation in the kitchen, I was just breathless. Totally rapt. Like all good teachers, she followed my lead, revealing more only if I asked more questions. And oh did I ask—I wanted to know about ghosts and communicating with the dead and *Is there such a thing as Soulmates? Because, like, I* totally *wanna meet my Soulmate.*

Their living room bookcase became my self-help library. I'd leave sleepovers with Ramtha books, *Messages from Michael*, and downloads from the Great White Brotherhood. One very special weekend, we drove to an out-of-the-way New Age bookstore in Michigan and my pal, with her mom's approval, handed me a book the size and look of my grandmother's Bible and said, *Here, I think you're ready for this.* It was *A Course In Miracles*. I put my favourite unicorn sticker on the back cover and wrapped it in my Journey concert t-shirt for the ride home.

Channeled material was my gateway drug to the New Age. It was a perfect introduction. Some of the material was far out and fantastical; it was engrossing, way better than the *Nancy Drew* series that I was bored with. And a lot of it was over my head and my capacity to focus.

Then, in my teens, I found Louise Hay's mega classic *You Can Heal Your Life,* and it opened up a whole new world for me about the body/mind connection. Louise was modelling in New York City when she discovered that she had cancer. With talk therapy to work through the pain of her childhood abuse, and with the power of positive thinking—mostly through affirmations—she completely healed herself. I learned about somatizing emotions, the power of what you tell yourself, and science of the mind. It was incredibly influential stuff at that time in my life.

It also kicked up my spiritually wide-eyed fears. I reckoned that I'd better clean up any resentment I had toward my parents in case it manifested as a tumour. *If I don't stop hating my dad for not letting me date The Hot Guy, I'm gonna get cancer!* That's what a teenage brain does with metaphysics. That's what any neophyte mind does with sweeping information:

it oversimplifies and makes it black or white. (And, by the way, I didn't really hate my dad. I secretly dated the Hot Guy anyway. And I didn't get a tumour.) Around the same time, I was being marched to confession with all the other little lambs in my Catholic school to ask for absolution from my sins. I wondered if repenting to God would keep me healthy. Or was it affirmations? Or the Hail Mary? Or crystal healing?

Between esoterics and a very well-organized religion, I had a buffet of guilt and fear to choose from—all of which I tried to resist with positive affirmations.

...

The economics of bettering

Being exposed to conflicting dogmas is one of the best things that can happen to you. Like Nietzsche said, "One must still have chaos within oneself, to give birth to a dancing star." Confusion always leads to clarity, and from there, you make your art in the world.

We fall for some lies to get down to our Truth.

All the falsifiers throughout the centuries, from the crusaders to charlatans, were just playing their roles in the unfolding of the bigger Truth. Some thought they had no choice but to pass down fabrications in order to earn the good favour of their deities. They wanted the riches of paradise that their gods promised in the afterlife. Some were true seekers wrestling with the big questions and earnestly trying to dispel the darkness with Love and Light. Others were trying on deception and power mongering for a karmic fit: *Hey! I know! Let's start an Inquisition!*

As humans, we've *slightly* increased our civility when it comes to how we defend and promote our beliefs. But just slightly. We've yet to make great strides of consciousness in our various Departments of Truth

Defense. We continue to slaughter and exile huge populations from their homelands over fundamentalist beliefs. Scores of us still follow religions that preach extreme intolerance. We kill for our gods. We bully non-believers. We wage war for what we believe to be true.

Many of us living relatively (or blatantly) privileged lives have created our own nouveau religion: Materialism. It's as pervasive as any of the major world religions. And we fight, and kill, and steal, and pillage, and lie for our right to profit and consume. Same shit, different deity—the deity of the dollar (or yen, or euro...). Our mass consumption has become a weapon of mass destruction—fashioned from lies about so-called success and happiness. These lies take a damaging toll on our self-esteem, and we keep trying to inflate our worth with more stuff, more attention, more stimulation. In the Cult of Materialism, reverence for simplicity and basic consideration is a courageous act.

A lie only has power when someone believes it. You need a congregation to have a church, fighters for an army, voters to get elected. You need buyers for wholesale lies. Lie-spreading requires widespread participation. It's not only that "they"—the government, or organized religions, or the media, or the educators—are cranking out non-truths. It's that all of us are paying—by choice—for a variety of deceptions with our money, time, and attention. We need to take individual responsibility for the beliefs that animate our lives. We need to acknowledge the ideals that are driving our choices.

So why do we choose certain beliefs over others? Especially when some beliefs are so damaging? Because they give us comfort. (And certain Truths are very uncomfortable.)

We crave the comfort of connection. We want that almost indefinable pleasure and ease that comes from feeling connected. We are psychologically and physiologically designed to be in community, and we'll believe and do preposterous things to feel attached, accepted, and approved of—especially if we can get the approval of a crowd. Essentially, we'll go along with lies so we can earn points from a perceived higher power. And too many of us think that other people's opinions *are* a higher power. We stoop and shrink to give more space to outside input. We become cautious and accommodating. We choose to believe that we are less powerful so that someone else can feel important when they approve of and "Love" us—but at least we get the Love we crave—not that it's real Love. If there ever was a vicious cycle...

If you think you're defective or in need of fixing (which is the biggest lie of all), you will most definitely attract lovers, teachers, preachers, and politicians who want to so-called "love" you, and "fix" you, and "lead" you. It's an economy of broken hearts and menders. Too many questions or too much self-sufficiency throws the salvation business out of balance. Emancipation and breakups would erupt, advertisers would go bankrupt, gods would topple. It would be self-reliance anarchy!

So I'm asking you:

Do your beliefs take your personal power into account?

Do your beliefs fuel your freedom?

Do you believe in yourself?

When paradigms go wrong

We naturally cycle through phases of righteousness when we find truths that resonate with us. Righteousness can be such a cool thing—that fiery belief in something, the willingness to go all out for your cause. And sometimes, it's totally obnoxious and your friends are, like, so over hearing about how The Empowerment Forum For the Immediate Enlightenment of Humanity changed your life, and how if they went, they'd totally get over their racket and be as expanded as you are.

We get preachy with the new stuff. We can also get angry and irrationally defiant. When I found out that veal came from baby cows kept in crippling crates to keep their meat tender, I protested family barbecues by aggressively eating salad and pontificating on animal cruelty. This didn't really help the baby cows, and once I almost fainted from hunger at work. Fear and zealotry are cohorts. If we need to feel more secure in our new beliefs, to have people's agreement affirm what we've chosen, then the soapbox is a great place to posture. It's also a great place to hide our fear that we could be wrong.

Zealousness can be a healthy passage to becoming more mature and effective. We go extreme with some beliefs, but with experience and perspective, we hopefully come to even keel. The growth process—and moderation—begins when we aren't as desperate for people's approval. And hopefully our friends hang in there with us during our righteous highs.

Timing counts for so much when it comes to discovering our Truth. As individuals, we're all just bumpin' alongside each other with various beliefs and opinions. God or Krishna (or science) knows, who you are as a Soul isn't always reflected back to you by the family or culture you were born into. All the black sheep, please raise your hands. We can grow up on a diet of lies, ideas that we later discover we're allergic to. Or, in a stroke of good fortune and/or excellent incarnational selection, we can grow up amongst life-affirming ideologies that build our muscles for the work we've come to do on the planet.

Either way, we can't use our upbringing or original culture to cruise-control through life. Eventually, we have to examine the beliefs that drive us and start asking some questions—lots of them. And never stop asking. Ever. Because the colossal, truly life-threatening problem happens when we take a lie and promote it to paradigm—our whole worldview. And there is some nasty fiction that finds its way into every kind of belief system and flavour of Faith, no matter how ancient, progressive, or holistic they may seem.

They are Fantastically Flawed Premises—and they keep us from self-acceptance, celebration, intimacy, and the true connection we crave. They are woven into the worst of dogmatic manipulation, marketing ploys, and political propaganda. And they drive our self-doubt and neurotic need for improvement and acceptance.

You might want to go light a candle right now and wear something white and flowy. Or crank some heavy metal and get ready to rage. We're going to have a demolition party for these Soul-sucking fabrications. Liberation is inevitable when you stop believing these lies.

Fantastically flawed premises
THE LIE OF INADEQUACY

> *I'm not telling you, 'You are good enough.' I am telling you,*
> *'You are complete and perfect before even the birth of time.'*
> – Mooji, *Give Me One Good Reason Why You Are Not the Self*

The Lie of Inadequacy says, "You were born defective, not good enough, *flawed.*"

Ha ha! Not even close.

Tragically, in many cultures this fallacy translates to, "You were born a girl...so you're inadequate." In others, it means that you incarnated into the wrong caste, or have the wrong shade of skin, or Love someone of the wrong gender, or some intersection of many of these alleged deficiencies. We can be force-fed the Lie of Inadequacy by social messaging and doctrines. Or we can inherit it like a genetic transference, the stories of being unworthy that get etched on our DNA, generation after generation.

Christianity bolsters the Lie of Inadequacy with the concept of Original Sin. Roman Catholics, classical Anglicans, Methodists, Mormons, and Jehovah's Witnesses all believe in some variation of "we come into this world soiled with sin." Makes it hard to get off to a good start, doesn't it?

In Grade Two at St. John's Catholic School, Father Flynn, who my dad said was "older than dirt 'n' Jesus," informed us all that we were "born with original sin on our foreheads." He was paying our classroom a visit to talk to us about our upcoming First Holy Communion. I was excited because I knew we'd get to practice taking communion with some unblessed wafers. I'd been rehearsing at home with Triscuit crackers, so finally getting to taste one of those real semi-sacred Jesus wafers was going to be a super duper treat. But alas, all the excitement I had was dashed by the somber news that day: I was born a sinner.

Excuse me? *But I was just a little baby girl–person, how could I have been bad yet?* I could not wrap my head around the concept. I brought my little paw to my forehead and tried to inconspicuously feel if there was, like, an original sinner-ness bump or indentation. Some proof of being marked (for life, evidently).

We have Adam to thank for this mess, since the fall of man, humanity's alleged state of sin, goes back to when Adam got with Eve and ate the apple from the tree of knowledge of good and evil. "For just as through the disobedience of one person the many were made sinners, so through the obedience of one the many will be made righteous." No pressure though.

Some Christians believe that original sin explains why so many disastrous and dark things—war, violence, suicide, suffering—happen in a world that was created by a perfect Godhead.

Even though we were created "in His image" (except for the perfection part, I guess?), we are sinners and He is absolved of the responsibility for the evils of the world. Hunh. (This would never happen with a female God figure, by the way. She'd just assume responsibility for her share of the sinnin' *and* she'd overcompensate for everyone else's bad deeds by working overtime and multitasking with good deeds. And then we'd all talk it through over lunch and make sure everything was copacetic.) In this scenario, God is off the hook (because He's omnipotent), but we are not off the hook of sin (because we are the opposite of omnipotent, apparently, which is impotent, which is not just a drag in bed but also means "helpless" or "worthless"). But it's supposedly all okay in the end—as in the end of our life—because we can implore God to save our sinning Souls.

If this seems confusing, it's because it's supposed to be. Oppressors use confusion to create reliance. This is a good time to mention that I'm not anti-Christian; I'm anti-oppression. I deeply adore Jesus Christ and the flame of his Love burns brightly in my heart. But we'll get to that later.

Matthew Fox (nope, not the hot guy from the *Lost* TV show) is an American priest and activist who works within a larger theology called "Creation Spirituality." In my mid-twenties, I danced to trance beat drums and didgeridoos at Fox's Cosmic Masses in San Francisco. Think: Holy Communion meets indigenous ritual, at a rave on a Sunday morning in a hotel ballroom. Bliss! I felt quenched by a Faith that was so fluid, and their translation of Christ's message seemed to be the least distorted that I'd found. I met with an admissions officer to talk about attending the ministerial program at Fox's University of Creation Spirituality. I wanted to be a really sexy young priest(ess) in contemporary communion with the world. But life had other plans, and I moved northwest to be with a brainy boy and start a business—an altogether different kind of mission.

Fox used to be a member of the Dominican Order within the Roman Catholic Church, but he was expelled for disobedient acts such as: referring to God as "The Mother," working too closely with Native American spiritual practices, and not condemning homosexuality. And! In an outrageous act of defiance, Father Fox preferred and promoted the concept of "Original Blessing" over Original Sin. "We burst into the world as 'Original Blessings,'" is how he put it. Not sinners. The only "sin" Fox recognizes is that of dualism—of seeing people and things as being separate from one another and God. His life's work has been to further a Faith that is rooted in our "original goodness."

Original goodness isn't the message that most of us get from our religious forebearers. What's it like to go through life thinking you're not quite enough? Well, most of us know the answer to that. We become chronic self-fixers or habitual strivers, always trying to get on the right side of Universal law.

You know what this looks like...maybe you're just weird in a world that worships "normal," safe, and secure. (Please, rock your weird; we all need it.)

Maybe your dad wanted a boy but you were a girl, so they named you Jamie and taught you to play baseball. Your folks clearly loved you but you felt like you got off on the wrong foot, and ever since Day One you've been either trying to sharpen your warrior nature or ooze feminine goddess goodness to make it all okay...to try to get on the good side of it all.

Or maybe you feel like there's a veil draped between your intentions and your staying power. It's gossamer and filmy, but it keeps you from holding on to whatever you catch. It's the subtle but smothering Lie of Inadequacy telling you that you don't deserve the abundance that comes to you, that you're here and what you want is way over there, on the good side of it all.

There's a beautiful scene in the movie *The Help*, where Viola Davis' character, Aibileen, the hired maid and nanny, holds her (very racist) employer's little girl in her arms, and says, "You is kind, you is smart, you is important." And the little sweetie pie recites it with her, "You is kind, you is smart, you is important." And that's the greatest gospel of original goodness I've ever heard.

You were born important. With full rights. Just for showing up. You are more than adequate; you are substantial. Worthy. Powerful. You are a blessing of original goodness.

THE LIE OF AUTHORITY

> *You become mature when you become the authority in your own life.*
> – Joseph Campbell

The Lie of Authority says, "You need someone else to validate your worth and your choices."

Hell no. Please no. Definitely...no.

If you really want to mess with people, call yourself a "spiritual authority." Whether it's true or false, it's one of the most magnetic, profoundly comforting, and almost-impossible-to-verify claims that a person can make.

If you really want to mess up your life, never question spiritual authorities.

The Information Age is a thrilling, unifying, empowering galvanizer of global progress. With all the communication and data streaming through the nervous system of the planet, it's an incredible time to be alive. It also means that just about anybody can get certified to be...a life coach.

A few tele-meetings and you too can become a certified lifestyle spiritual empowerment coachy expert authority. Look, I'm one hundred percent in favour of life coaches and spiritual guides. Obviously. I've had dozens of them. Spent thousands of dollars on them. I even have my own workshop curriculum that I license to amazing coaches and yoga teachers. I think every woman should have a room of her own, as Virginia Woolf declared, and, I'd like to add, a life coach.

But we're becoming experts at being experts in things we're not really experts in. Shallow knowledge, limited experience. To be clear, we're living in the Age of Information, not the age of wisdom. Wisdom comes from lived and earned experience. You went through the experience, you had your own awakenings and insights—you developed wisdom—you didn't just download the PDF. With his classic badassery, Henry Rollins sums it up: "Knowledge without mileage equals bullshit."

Labels can be useful calling cards. A shaman is a shaman, the CEO is the CEO—it's good to know who thinks they're in charge of what. Authority labels can create a lot of separation when ideologies are at play. In a radio interview I was introduced as a "spiritual teacher." I couldn't interject quickly enough. *Oh, please, no. I'm not a spiritual teacher. I talk about spiri-*

tual things that might be useful, but I'm not a spiritual teacher. This isn't false modesty. I'm not, and I don't want the karma that comes with that label—which is a whole lot of projection and pressure to be flawless. I mean, I like to think I'm the Beyoncé kind of flawless, I woke up like this and all. Have attitude, will travel. But I'm not out to be an impeccable practitioner or instructor of anything. I'm a seeker who writes about what I find. And maybe, on just the right day, I can help you flatten your learning curve. If I've got anything to say, it's this: **you are the authority on you.**

NOBODY knows better than you what's right for you. NOBODY. Let me say what I really mean: NOBODY. Advice? Get some. Oracles? Consult them. Friends? Worship them. Actual gurus? Honour them. Final say? YOU. All you. No matter what. No matter how psychic that psychic is, or how rich the business consultant is, or how magical the healer, or bendy the yoga instructor. All that experts offer you is data for you to take into *consideration.* YOU are the centrifugal force that must filter, interpret, and give meaning to that data. Your body knows. Your heart knows. Your mind will help you act on what you know.

My guiding philosophy about any philosophy is: **take what you want and leave the rest.** There is no one ideology or teacher who is one hundred percent right. Even though they may be vastly, deeply experienced, experience is based on the past. We can't always look for precedent to inform our future. How they did it, what worked then...that was them then, this is you in the now.

Will there be times when you should heed external advice? Yep. Plenty of them. Because when your good, wise friend says, "Have you lost your mind?!"—well, maybe you have. But you have to make the final call. Your Soul has a plan. And your Soul is your authority.

THE LIE OF AFFILIATION

> *Freethinkers are those who are willing to use their minds without*
> *prejudice and without fearing to understand things that clash*
> *with their own customs, privileges, or beliefs. This state of*
> *mind is not common, but it is essential for right thinking.*
> – Leo Tolstoy

The Lie of Affiliation says, "Groupthink is good think." A byproduct of The Lie of Authority, we could also call this The Lie of Being Cool.

Yikes. Nooo. Danger, danger.

Flashback: I'm in one of those personal development workshops where the Apparently Evolved Guy Who Has More Money Than Everyone in the Room is working his neural-linguistic programming kung fu to get participants to share their deepest secrets with a group of utter strangers. (What? You were there? Thought I recognized you.)

"Who wants to share next?" asks The Leader Guy into the microphone. There are only thirty of us in a small conference room. He doesn't require a mic to be heard, but, you know, spectacle. He doesn't wait for anyone to volunteer. He zooms in on Pablo. Because it's obvious that Pablo is scared shitless. Now, I naturally gravitate to the sweet, scared guys in group settings because I'm a natural mama bear and it's easy to make the kind and quivery guys laugh. It's a win-win. So I was sitting next to Pablo, noticing that he'd balled up tissue in both hands to help with his sweating palms. I looked at him to say, *Dude, it's your call.*

Leader Guy walks Pablo through his proprietary and trademark-pending series of spirit-cracking questions and, right on cue, Pablo gets into his childhood story. An obese and verbally abusive mother, living in a house of total squalor and infestation, being sexually abused by a relative. It went on. It got worse. Unspeakably (unless you're in a group workshop) worse. That abuse resulted in all kinds of neuroses and obsessive-compulsive behaviour in adulthood. He cried through his story, and all the emotionally available people in the room joined in with him. Leader Guy walked him through the final phase of the Q&-gruelling-A. And then, I kid you not, he signaled all of us to group-hug Pablo while the workshop DJ in the back of the room played Wynonna Judd's cover of Foreigner's "I Wanna Know What Love Is." You can't make this shit up, but you can pay $795.00 plus accommodations for it.

At dinner, one of the spirit-intoxicated attendees says to me, "Isn't this wonderful?! That sharing that Pablo did is going to change his life!" I looked up from my bowl of quinoa and said, "Maybe. But I think when he gets back to work on Monday he's going to regret the shit outta this." Because some things are too sacred for a fluorescent-lit hotel conference room. There are some things you should only tell your qualified therapist or your best friend in the sanctity of private space, when you're truly ready—and *that's* how the real healing happens. With respect and skill, not manipulation.

But groups get it out of us, don't they? We tend to love the comfort of belonging, even if it's belonging to miserable company. And leaders take the heat off of us to do the work ourselves, if only temporarily. All we have to do is spill the beans and cry, and we're welcomed right in. But a few days later, we wake up with a wicked spiritual hangover.

Wanting to be affiliated with a cause or group can get more convoluted when we're getting together for spiritual reasons. It's not like we're meeting to strategize Ponzi schemes or kidnappings. We're getting together to make the world a better place, man. Who's gonna stand up in the "How to Be More Loving" retreat to say, "The workshop leader is being mean to people and this is total bullshit"? That would not seem very *wuving*.

We experience group enchantment to define our individuality. We enlist, we play, we promote, we wake up, we leave the flock. And then, we go find where we truly belong. **May you find your tribe and Love them hard.**

it takes courage to change your beliefs

3
TRUTHFULLY SEEKING
How wisdom happens (hint: paradoxically)

How wonderful that we have met with a paradox.
Now we have some hope of making progress.
– Niels Bohr

Ask more questions

AROUND THE AGE of eight, I came across the concept of eternity—it's the ultimate religious sales pitch, eternity. Serious business. It's the "take no prisoners" of all binary choices: would you prefer an eternity in heaven, or would you rather an eternity in hell? *Hunh. Let me mull it over. How long do I have to get back to you?*

So there I am, sitting on the living room couch after Hamburger Helper and an episode of *Happy Days* (the good phase, right before Chachi took off with Joanie), and I'm ruminating, as eight-year-olds do, on "eternity." I stretched my malleable little mind as far as it could go. *A time without end,* I repeated to myself, using priest language that I'd memorized verbatim.

That means that eternity is forever and ever and ever and ever and ever and ever and ever and ever and ever and ever and ever and endless forevers and evers. As the *ever and evers* kept going, my eyes filled with tears. I could not handle the magnitude. Eternity scared the crap out of me. See? Very effective recruitment tool.

What I was too young to articulate was this counter question: who wants an eternity of *anything*? Even if it's heavenly, it's going to get old. That prospect seemed so bleak to me that it forced me into Faith (as religious ultimatums are engineered to do). I had to have Faith that, surely, God must have something better in store for us than being permanently parked in heaven. *There must be field trips, at least.*

Who doesn't want to believe that if you do all the right things, you'll be rewarded for it? Of course the big theories appeal to us: they're simple and direct. So right or so wrong. So *explained*. But there's a problem with acceptance of wholesale beliefs from any worldview.

No questioning = no growth. Your curiosity is the bloodstream of your own spirituality. Curiosity carries nourishment to your Faith—the heart of your spirit. The more curious you are about how life works, the more present you will be in your life.

Curiosity is different than desperately seeking, though there's a time for that—a.k.a., crisis time. When I'm in pain, when I want what I want, then I want to get the right answers and solutions, stat. And I used to try anything. Feng shui to get the money flowing, chakra clearing to get the mojo moving, another clairvoyant to tell me when and how it's all going to manifest.

Curiosity is slightly more patient and confident. A friend of mine, an avowed Buddhist in the Shambhala line, was prepping me for a retreat I'd just signed up for. "Question everything the lama says. Buddhists love that shit." Got it. "Oh, and if he asks, tell him you have no intention whatsoever of taking vows—that'll totally turn him on." Noted: turn on the lama with intellectual rebelliousness.

The immaculacy of all great teachings is questionable. So we *should* question it—all of it. Actively. Constantly.

Questioning your teachers is not a betrayal of them, or your God, or guru, or your favourite seer. It is not an act of cynicism or mistrust. It's self-respecting optimism. It's a belief in your right to do what's best for you and Faith that you'll figure out what that is.

Spectrums of seeking

There is no such thing as "the truth" that can be stated. In other words, ask the question: "What is the true position of the stars in the Big Dipper?" Well, it depends on where you're looking at them from.
– Alan Watts

The Viennese philosopher Martin Buber said, "The world is not comprehensible, but it is embraceable." The thirst for knowledge is *such* an incredible characteristic of humans. We instinctively and relentlessly seek the Truth knowing that it might very well be unknowable within the limits of our mind. And yet, still...we seek.

Relative. Objective. Subjective. Absolute. Unknowable. Who knows. The Truth.

Incomprehensible. Mind-bogglingly vast. Stunning, sometimes terrifying, luminous, galvanizing, sweetly enveloping, healing, ultimately liberating, unfathomably deeply pleasing, gorgeously, divinely impeccable *Truth*.

Don't you want some of *that*? I do.

I'm an absolutist. I believe in one Truth. Except, I don't think any of us know what that Truth is. This makes me a fairly open-minded absolutist, which of course I think is the best kind. Righteous, yet...*flexible.*

I believe that there is a universal, all-pervasive Truth that architects Life. I believe in its magnificent genius. I believe that we all originate from that source—everything. I sense my creative power. I can recall a place where the "we" of humanity is the "I" that is God. I recollect a choice when "the we that is I that is God" decided to burst out into individual sparks of Light—Souls—a big bang of consciousness. We went into the cosmic wilderness by choice, an intentional adventure to re-member our way back home and evolve along the way. *It was and is the ultimate creative act—because Life lives to create.*

I think of my human mind as a **transmitter of Light**. (And what an amazing capacity that we humans have—to "think" about our minds!) Imagine that you've got on a magic helmet. It's more like a techno-turbo helmet-crown. A feminized, more cosmic version of something Iron Man might wear. (If only there were more women superheroes featured in Hollywood. If only filmmakers could conceive of a female tech-genius billionaire who wanted to kick some peacekeeping ass. If only we could entertain that all humans have fourth dimensional powers. If only. But I digress.)

This Light-transmitting helmet-crown pulls down esoteric knowledge from the ethers and translates it so the physical brain can process that Light into thoughts, words, ideas, and ultimately, your actions. The mind is a Truth filter. And like all filters, the mind has limited, but always expandable, capacities. It can only handle a certain amount of Light at a time. Too much Truth/Light could, very literally, *blow your mind.*

I wonder about all the people throughout time who have been committed to psychiatric wards, the "mad" artists and those diagnosed as delusional or schizophrenic. How many of them weren't chemically imbalanced or suffering a psychopathy, but rather, experiencing a spiritual transmission that was overloading their circuits? Who of the diagnosed and disregarded might actually be speaking Truth, or communicating inter-dimensionally?

You also need to consider the reverse: How many of the so-called sane and socially accepted people in positions of leadership or profit-making who claim connection with the Divine are actually speaking spirit-oppressing, harmful nonsense?

With God, Goddess, the Soul and the Universe being so unfathomable but magnificent, I imagine that a mere drop of such pure power on my tongue would have me reeling. Combustion. Dissolution. I'd melt into the great ecstatic is-ness, smiling deliriously all the way. Which makes me thankful for the restrictions of this third dimension and the suitcase I call a body. Combustion can wait. I dig being on the Earth-plane.

Einstein said that time exists only so everything doesn't happen all at once. We need to be fed the Truth a bite at a time, revelation after sweet revelation. And when we're hungry again, we ask for more.

Your mission, should you choose to accept it, is to increase your capacity to receive and transmit Light. This is what it means to "raise your frequency," to "tune in." You're adjusting your dials to Truth Radio (and the hits will keep coming).

Truth has spectrums. Sequences. Levels. And each dose of Truth expands us, increasing our capacity to receive and give more Truth and Light. Seek and you shall find...one layer of Truth at a time. Every experience we have in life, even the missteps, and especially the bliss, is a step closer to that sacred radiance. **We are all waking up in the same direction.**

Changing contradictions

What did you used to believe in that you now think is ridiculous?

Here, I'll go first: Soulmates. I used to think there was only one person for every person. An exquisite match of values and ethereal and earthly connectedness that would magnetize two Souls together in unbreakable union. Now? Now I think "The One" is the one because you say they are.

I'm gonna make you The One. You're it 'cause I said so. And that very intentional selection is so much more romantic and powerful than waiting on the Fates to deliver a one-in-seven-billion person to your door.

I believed in destiny. Now I'm into free will. I used to think I could heal someone with my Love. Now I know it takes a lot more than Love. Most of the time, people have to heal themselves.

It takes courage to change your beliefs. Beliefs are so intertwined with the people around us; we are accepted or rejected based on our beliefs. Beliefs keep our private world in order. Change what you believe and you change your life.

> *That's your responsibility as a person, as a human being—to constantly be updating your positions on as many things as possible. And if you don't contradict yourself on a regular basis, then you're not thinking.*
> – Malcolm Gladwell

Perhaps the Truth is absolute and fixed; even so, we are not—we are moving through space and time, seeing it from different angles.

I want to burn everything I've ever written before this morning. Today, I look at some of my prior offences/opinions, and I just roll my eyes and think, *Oh gawd, Danielle.* But that's what I felt then and it might still serve someone where they're at now. You may stand for something your whole life—you've been going on and on about this principle or standard that you hold so dear—and then, one day, you do something that's completely counter to what you've been preaching. You do something musketeer-like and brave: You make an exception to your own rule. And it makes perfect sense. You're not a hypocrite; you're just alive to your life in the moment—ever-changing.

We do not grow absolutely, chronologically. We grow sometimes
in one dimension, and not in another, unevenly. We grow partially.
We are relative. We are mature in one realm, childish in another.
The past, present and future mingle and pull us backward, forward,
or fix us in the present. We are made of layers, cells, constellations.

– Anaïs Nin

We are big spirits with human shortcomings. And if we're being our authentic selves, we will be walking, breathing, dancing, tweeting contradictions.

We can have strong, yogic bodies and still crumble when we think we've disappointed someone. We can be incredibly generous with our money and possessions but highly controlling of the time we give to others. Vulnerable lovers, ruthless business people. Public introverts. Bacon-loving vegetarians.

We think contradictions indicate hypocrisy. But hypocrisy is actually feigning to hold certain morals when you yourself don't conform to them. And even so, sometimes hypocrisy is a lesson in strengthening our integrity. Somehow we got the idea that being whole is about being perfectly consistent. I'd rather we be perfectly honest. We can't put parts of ourselves aside in thinking it will make us more wholesome. Crushing our so-called vices, being robotically disciplined and formulaically polite can stifle our power. "We have to be careful that in throwing out the devil," said Nietzsche, "that we don't throw out the best part of ourselves."

If we can't treasure our contradictions, then how will we prove the value of a spirituality that can accommodate rage, and a body politic that can show mercy? Or a generous capitalism, and a unified diversity of beliefs?

Bless this mess

Every religion and doctrine has its purists to protect it. They endeavour to preserve the originality of the sacred teachings. Often, their secondary job is to go forth and dispense that information to a new audience. Some teachings are distributed as widely as possible, like yoga or Buddhism brought from the East to the West. Some wisdom is passed down through lineages and bloodlines. Some of it is codified or kept hidden so that only esoteric practitioners with the right intentions can put it to good use.

Truth dispensation is problematic business. Teachings cross continents, millennia of shifting cultures, and a mashup of human motives and agendas. History is usually recorded by the victors of the era, and the dominant race or gender. And if those biases weren't enough to limit perspective, the facts, such as they are, get translated and re-translated through multiple languages. I think if Jesus ran a branding campaign these days, his slogan would be: *That's not what I meant by that.*

Remember the telephone game from when you were a kid? You whisper into the ear of the girl next to you, "Let's run in the field and pick daisies," then she whispers it to the boy beside her, who then mumbles it to the next kid, and so on. By the time the message makes it around the circle, it's: "Bet one of you is sick and crazy." Even as we try to keep it straight, humans distort things, especially when we urgently want to get our point across.

If you're overly attached to your Truth, hypocrisy is a hazard. Because the Truth is never black and white—it's encompassing. It's and/BOTH. Puritanism is a trap for being offended and offensive. When we cling to our principles, we shrink our vision to myopic proportions where there is no give and take, only preaching. Nationalists who hang people for burning flags. Capitalists who deplete resources. Light preachers who operate in the dark.

I deeply respect purists who want to protect sacred information—what noble work that can be in a world that distorts so much. But I have a problem with righteous purists—the puritanical heavies who create division and shame with their arrogant inflexibility in the name of their god, race, nation, history, gender.

When we turn away from each other, we turn away from our own Souls.

When you combine personal ambition with misinformation, you get propaganda. We go from authentic Esoteric Truth to Disney-fied gimmicks for getting ahead in life—always ahead. Authentic mystical movements are turned into a collage of truth and lies. It's a mess. But you know what? It's a beautiful mess that we can't and shouldn't try to avoid. We are humans having a relationship with God (Life, Light, whichever term works for you) and relationships are *complicated*. We are fumbling our way toward ecstasy.

Truth distortion is part of Truth clarification. If we accept that the dilution, pollution, and misappropriation of Truth is inevitable, then we'll be a lot more compassionate with ourselves and each other.

Traditions are being lost. The Truth is being twisted up and watered down. I look at it as a necessary, albeit risky, guessing game to help us learn to decipher Truth for ourselves. What stays? What goes? What do we fight for? When do we stop fighting? Less worshipping of outer sources and more discernment of spiritual information means that we learn to feel what's true for ourselves. When you're walking in the dark, you can either sit down and wait for someone to give you directions, or you can get extra-sensory and see for yourself.

Wisdom is paradoxical

True wisdom usually holds and *transcends* opposing points of view. Wisdom knows that there is always an exception to the rule, that there is a time and place, and that case-by-case is divine protocol.

If you can comfortably hold your paradoxes, you're going to be just fine. Because I'm suggesting that you:

1. Love yourself first and foremost *and* Include the world in your loving (and then get off your ass and be more selflessly engaged)
2. Raise your standards *and* Be more flexible and accommodating
3. Forgive *and* Don't forget
4. Honour spiritual traditions *and* Be your own guru
5. Be open-hearted *and* Have clear, strong boundaries
6. Be understanding *and* Don't take any shit
7. Have a vision *and* Go with the flow
8. Trust *and* Do the work
9. Get real *and* Be idealistic
10. Be steadfast in your Truth *and* Make all kinds of exceptions
11. Have strong preferences *and* Be easy to please
12. Lead with your heart *and* Your head
13. Own your extraordinariness *and* Your ordinariness

Because it's up to you *and* we're all in this together.

And hey...we have all the time in the world, but this is urgent.

Create
where you
belong

4
HEALING INSTINCTS

Mixing our own medicine
(it's all an experiment)

There is a time for everything,
and a season for every activity under the heavens...
– Ecclesiastes 3:1

Between worlds

O N MY OWN healing journey, I've called on psychologists, Buddhists, the Super Woos, and medical professionals (both traditional and "alternative"). There's a lot of overlap amongst them, of course. But here's what I've learned: each form of assistance is, on its own, terrifically helpful—and utterly incomplete. If you want to take your life to the next level, you need backup from multiple perspectives and traditions. **You're complex. And your support system needs to be as multi-faceted, robust, and weird as you are.**

Boldly going

When I was going through something (and when are we not going through something?), I'd circle back to my beloved therapist, Michael B., for some of his wisdom and witnessing. In addition to our cherished interaction, I was always exchanging the names of energy workers on the side with my friends. It was like trading mystical baseball cards.

Oooh! I've got this guy who'll clean your chakras and does Soul imprinting stuff. What's Soul imprinting? *Dunno, but we did this journey thing and I cleared so much shit.* Why don't you tap that shit out? EFT, Emotional Freedom Technique. I tap before all my meetings now, really helps with my anxiety. I'm teaching my kids to tap. *I need more than tapping. I want like, an exorcism of all the bullshit.* I know! What about that healer who used to be a psychiatrist who does the Divine Light sessions? She has dream visions for you the night before, and then you work with your guides to clear your stuff out. *Now we're talking. Can you text me her number?*

I felt like I was cheating on my psychotherapist with my energy worker. And I was concerned that my energy worker was going to be hurt if I wanted to talk things through with my therapist. And would my naturopath be mad if I surrendered to my MD and took some antibiotics? And forget about my gyno: she diagnosed me as a total flake when I told her that—*gasp*—acupuncture and ashwagandha were all I needed. "Ashwa what? Well, I've heard acupuncture can be moderately useful," she said, arms folded.

There wasn't one type of practitioner or counsellor who could help me navigate my entire course of self-care. And the more mystical my learning experiences became, the more I felt like I was going to have to go it alone.

My girlfriend referred me to a trauma release massage therapist after I was in a car accident. "Tell me vhat happened," she asked in her thick Swiss accent. "The other guy ran a red light and t-boned me. My car was totalled. I got out and stood in the rain waiting for the cops to come. My hips and shoulder are bruised from the seat belt but I'm fine. I just kind of...walked away." Pause. "Iz zat all?" she asked, slightly suspecting that I was withholding something. I clammed up. "Yep. That's it," I nodded quickly, biting my lip.

I could not even begin to explain to her that milliseconds before impact I heard a voice that told me, "Everything is going to be okay." And "okay" meant that I wasn't going to be hurt in this accident. And that I'd be well and held *in this entire lifetime*. And that my son (who fortunately was not in the car with me) would also be okay *for this entire lifetime*.

And I found myself *floating in the most peculiar way*...in deep, ink-blue space amongst luminous clear-white stars—it was the same space I've visited during some meditations and orgasms. And I wasn't a star. And I wasn't space. I was me, with God, and "me" was "we" was "I." And everything was so blissfully, peacefully, *perfect*. There isn't a word or a library of words to describe the sheer perfection of it all.

It was so quiet, that I could hear...magnificence.

That all happened in linear seconds. But I felt like I was in space for hours. I could have stayed for weeks.

Who was going to help me process *that ride*? Maybe science, in this case. A place I usually turn to last for answers. Astronauts who have been to space often have a spontaneous spiritual experience called the Overview Effect. They talk about the vastness, that sudden macro understanding of the planet and how perfect, fragile, and breathtaking it is. With that "God's-eye view," they understand how we all belong to each other, and they report that it's a simultaneously peaceful and lonely experience.

I let the massage therapist work on my hip flexors. Then I went to my shrink to analyze my feelings about what happened after the accident: the heartbreakingly beautiful exchange I had with the timid man who caused the crash, followed by an excruciating conflict that same night with my then-husband. And then, of course, I did a session with my energy worker to see if any trauma from all of the related events was lurking in my cells.

But I kept the real story to myself. I wanted to let it live in the centre of my centre where my inner space had met all of space, to be untouched by analysis, to be utterly and completely *known*. And I wondered if maybe

I'd write about it someday, quietly. Which, you know, can be the best therapy of all.

Takes a village

The main event in my Cirque du (in)Sanity has been therapy. It cycles in and out with different tribulations and big life questions, sometimes with a few years' gap in between attending. The great thing about being a self-help-centric female is that if I'm not in therapy, for sure one of my girlfriends is. There's an incredible phenomenon that happens among women, and it's perhaps the greatest application of our innate mavenry: when one of us goes to therapy, we *all* get some therapy. The download of one shrink session shared between Soul Sisters gets a ton of mileage. *Oh my God that is a good one, I'm going home to ask my babe that same question tonight! Holy shit, that is some breakthrough stuff, I need to call my mother. So* that's *why we're both so screwed up—makes total sense.*

The Merriam-Webster dictionary defines psychotherapy as *the treatment of mental or emotional illness by talking about problems rather than using medicine or drugs.* Now, my girlfriends and I have never thought of ourselves as definitively mentally or emotionally ill, though amongst the girl squad, we have been highly anxious, clinically depressed, obsessive compulsive, and moderately narcissistic. We just thought we were, you know, working through some karma.

In my experience, psychotherapy is eighty percent talking and twenty percent crying—and that snot-fest kind of crying is what makes all the difference. I went to therapy to be witnessed. I went to examine the motives of my choices for their integrity. I needed someone to tell me that I was sane, that I was special, and that I wasn't all that special. In the most practical sense, I just wanted someone to carry my pain with me for 60 paid minutes so I could catch my breath.

Side note: I've learned that therapy works better when you feel liked, or even truly loved, by your therapist. Of course, if you work with a shrink long enough, you're bound to project all of your nasty interpersonal hang-ups on them—*You're just like my older sister!*—and then you need to get another therapist to do therapy for your therapy. But generally, kindness and respect are a great foundation for healing. I stopped working with one therapist after a few sessions because I felt basically disliked. And that was exactly the therapeutic lesson I needed to translate into every area of my life at that time: if you don't like how someone treats you, get up and leave.

Psychologists & Buddhists

Psychology doesn't distinguish between beneficial and harmful emotions like, say, Buddhism does. Where psychology approaches most (but not all) "negative" emotions as fodder for healthy development, Buddhism takes the stance that some emotions must be dissolved and transformed because they are at the very root of our suffering. In even minor degrees, states of craving and hatred are considered afflictive and toxic. So while your shrink might say that it's good to feel your feelings of seething hatred, your rinpoche would say you need to notice how the hatred arises within your consciousness and not identify with it. I Love both points of view, which boil down to: *hey, it's all good, but some of it is really, really bad.*

The Super Woos

The Super Woos take into consideration the mystical forces of life, from synchronicity to cosmology, and evoke information and healing skills from other dimensions, or at least acknowledge that those dimensions influence our material lives.

In the silo of the Super Woos I include: intuitives, shamans and medicine people, channelers, mediums, angel communicators, Akashic records readers, and energy workers. My favourite of the Super Woos are pluralistic: they believe in, and usually draw on for themselves, a diversity of religions. Super Woos tend to be incredibly curious and inclusive, because they have had to weave together their own brand of spirituality. They are naturally weird, often wonderfully skilled, and due to the etheric nature of their skillset, it can be very difficult to discern the well-intentioned Super Woos from the misaligned ones. Which of course is all part of getting spiritually schooled—*discernment.*

Bio healers

The western medical establishment defines "alternative medicine" as any practice that doesn't come from evidence gathered using the scientific method. I've come to understand "alternative" healing to mean: "When the mainstream, profit-centric medical establishment fails you, you will seek out healing techniques that have been working for thousands of years as an *alternative*." I'm not anti-allopathic medicine or anti-pharma; I call on MDs and meds when I've tried everything else. But the fact that the medical establishment reduces the huge global spectrum of ancient healing modalities to the term "alternative" tells us how limited its viewpoint is. Very, very limited.

Functional Medicine is a great middle road between the West and the East. It's a brilliant systems-oriented approach to healing that creates a partnership between healer and patient and addresses the underlying causes of disease instead of just medicating the symptoms. My Functional Medicine doctor can prescribe everything from conventional medicine to licorice tea, she preaches about the inflammatory evils of sugar, and has an abiding respect for energy work.

In a psychotherapeutic context, head meds only enter the picture with psychiatrists and medical doctors—psychologists can't prescribe medication. It has always struck me as absurd (and ludicrous and irresponsible and highly dangerous) that MDs, trained extensively on the biological functions of the human body but much less so on the workings of the mind, can dispense psychotropic drugs to patients without any extensive therapeutic interaction.

At a university house party, a new friend shared that she'd started taking Prozac for her depression (and as a result she couldn't orgasm). "Well, what did your therapist say?" I asked her. "I've never been to a therapist," she replied. Naïvely, I asked, "Well, how'd you get the Prozac?" Simple. "I told my doctor I was depressed and he wrote me a prescription." I took a breath to keep my face soft but I was having a hard time understanding this. "A *medical* doctor?" I asked. "Ya, the guy who does my pap smears." I couldn't let it go—and we needed to get that poor girl having orgasms again. "How often do you go to this guy?" I gently pressed. She shrugged, "Once or twice a year."

Antidepressants can be the best course of action for breaking painful cycles and getting much needed respite from severe depression. But the fact that one in four women in the United States alone is taking antidepressants makes me want to weep.

I once had a public conversation about this with Dr. Sara Gottfried, a Harvard-trained MD. She said, "We know that most of those women—the one in four—they're struggling with stress, with hyper-vigilance, with cortisol. Fifty percent of people with depression have high cortisol. We know that twenty percent of people with depression have a problem with their thyroid—a slow thyroid—and often no one bothered to check those levels. We also know that a lot of this has to do with being in that less resourceful, reactive, triggered place too much of the time, and not able to declare how it is that you want to feel—which is where Desire Mapping comes in." Yes, ahem, some self-help books can come in very handy.

Dr. Sara went on: "We also live in a culture that's determined to throw a prescription pill at the problems that we have, yet we're not getting to the root cause. Let's start with the biology along with the work on the psyche." Applause!

On the other end of the self-care range are the stubborn self-help warriors (I'll raise my hand). "I'm just going to do some visualizations and up my echinacea," you tell your friend during your second week of coughing up chunks of your lungs. "I'm just processing some stuff." And through the other end of the phone your buddy yells, "GO TO THE DOCTOR! YOU NEED DRUGS!" You crawl to the clinic and wonder what took you so long to get there.

One of my closest friends is a gifted intuitive and Ayurvedic practitioner. Her newly minted ex-husband was dishing out one shocking surprise after another. She was preparing for their son's wedding, where she'd have to be civil to her ex and his whole snooty clan. We were strategizing on how she'd survive the festivities without stabbing anyone or going fetal on the dance floor. "I don't know if I can hold it together much longer," she said, quivering and angry all at once. Context: this is a woman who sees angels in the grocery store, who dreams prophetically, who has healed herself from breast cancer—twice. She's a contemporary, real-deal Priestess. "You can do this," I affirmed. Then she spit it out: "I think I should get some Xanax to take before the reception." Silence. Based on our mutual history of self-help bravado, she was probably expecting me to suggest that she steer clear of the mood drugs and just do some mantras on the drive to the country club. "Fuckin' do it!" I cheered. "Get the meds and just get through the ordeal." There's a time and place for everything. Knowing the right time and the right place is how you become your own healer.

In summary: psychology sorts out how your parents screwed you up when you were a child. Buddhism looks at how your mind can transmute your emotions about how screwed up you are. Spiritualists look at the past lives in which you and your parents were mutually screwed up, and how you can use that knowledge to become a more loving person in this lifetime. And if all that fails, call a doctor.

Living into the healing

> There isn't one medicine that alone will cure your ills. Not a single theory exists that explains everything, no sage who is always right. We're innovating how we heal, and in doing so we're creating the world in which we live. How we live, how we heal...they are inextricable.

We are making this up as we go. When you're on the cusp of your own consciousness, you will feel like a lonely, lost astronaut—ever in awe of what you're finding.

We are revising the requirements of what it means to be a whole person. Cosmic philosopher Jean Houston describes this as the **possible human**:

"One senses ebullience in her bones and an appetite for celebrating life. And wherever in the past that wounding has occurred, she can visit that time in her mind as the wiser version of her former self and bring understanding, compassion, and wisdom to the occasion... She is one about whom we might say that, 'The human heart can go to the lengths of God.'"

Psychological measurements can't plumb the depths of the Soul, and they certainly can't measure spiritual attainment. There is some karma that even Buddhism can't explain away. We need the Goddess, and we need antibiotics. We need magical thinking, magical spells, and practical techniques to cure fear and disease.

To heal, we need to look everywhere for our Light, turning outward and inward, to the north, south, east, and west. Walking in many worlds at once and, of course, bringing our findings back home—creating where we belong.

love yourself like it's your job

5
FULL OF YOURSELF

The curiosities of self-hatred,
and the only guarantee of self-Love

Secretly not nice

Y OU'RE BRIGHT. YOU know who you are, and you're committed to knowing more. You're becoming more successful all the time (and you're smart enough to know that "success" is a relative term). You're a generally stable, confident, compassionate citizen. You practice mindful speech, you send Light to the people who piss you off, you get regular massage treatments.

And yet...you kind of hate yourself. You'd never say it out loud, but just a little bit, somewhere in there, there's some certifiable self-loathing.

I used to think that my self-criticism was part of being self-aware and self-referencing, an essential component to having a moral conscience. I preferred to call it *critiquing*. Sounded more *je ne sais quoi*. I thought that pushing myself hard to be a better person was a spiritual responsibility.

I assumed this was because of all the Virgo I had in my chart. Five planets in Virgo in fact. (My sun sign is Gemini, which explains why I'm such a superlative and modest communicator.) But my non-Virgo New Age friends were just as hard on themselves. This was never more apparent than with their daily tasks. As many women will attest, the greatest, most monumental trigger of self-criticism in the history of lady-kind is...Our Fucking To-Do Lists.

Contemporary women revere their lists like Moses loved his stone tablets. They are directions to the Promised Land. The thrill of crossing something off: check, check, and *check*. Mmmmm, feels so good. So good that you might write stuff down that you've already done just so you can cross it off (yep, you got it bad). Like any addiction, the to-do list is destined to lose its thrill when it rules us. I looked at my Listus Maximus and thought, *With all this psychotherapy, and reiki, and yoga, I barely have time for myself.* Snort.

My list started feeling like a row of soldiers shouting at me. I decided to track it for two days, to take a candid inventory of everything my to-do list was *really* saying to me. Once I started paying attention, that background noise became awfully loud. Its refrain, on repeat: **I sort of suck because I should...**

Go to yoga more. Not watch YouTube videos of baby pandas and Prince interviews while I'm writing about subjects of great import. Be more informed about world politics. Meditate every morning, and for much longer. Be more Loving. Be less judgmental and confrontational about crap customer service. Lose ten pounds (really, lose fifteen)—do so by eating more protein but not meat, but if I have to eat meat, make sure it's free-range and local. But I'd rather not eat meat, but then where am I gonna get easy protein? Be more Loving. Be more grateful and show more gratitude to everyone in the whole world. Send thank you cards to the readers who send gifts—make sure they're handwritten and sent within a week. Be more inclined to socialize. Be less critical of all the bad New Age websites with Comic Sans typeface. Be more Loving. Forgive her for not forgiving me. Be more Loving. Pay more attention to my kid—is he getting too much screen time? I should really be more Loving.

Not so Loving, is it? It's a hot pile of loathsome shitty shoulds underneath a lot of halo-polishing, that's what it is.

As seasoned Soul Seekers, the necessity of healthy self-esteem is in our awareness, at least. *And yet...* Hating yourself. Could there be a heavier, shame-soaked, cringe-inducing concept? Hatred. Hate of self. You hating... you?

How could you think of yourself this way?

In 1990, there was a small gathering of psychologists, scientists, and meditators who came together with the Dalai Lama to explore the topic of healing emotions. Sharon Salzburg was there—she's a much-adored writer on lovingkindness and happiness, and the co-founder of the Insight Meditation Society in the U.S. Their poignant interaction at the meeting is now legendary.

She asked him, "Your Holiness, what do you think about self-hatred?" Apparently His Holiness looked startled, leaned over to his translator, and emphatically and repeatedly asked for a translation of "self-hatred." Finally, he looked back to Sharon, and asked, "Self-hatred...what is that?"

Hold up. His Holiness the Dalai Lama, who is considered to be the incarnation of the Bodhisattva of Compassion, didn't get the concept of self-loathing—something that so many of us westerners know all too well? *You know, DOWN on yourself, man. We* live *this way.* When I first heard about this event, I thought, *Doesn't everyone hate themselves to some degree, like, isn't it just a universal human affliction?* Apparently not.

Also present at that meeting of great minds was meditation teacher and author Jack Kornfield, who adds to the story. "Then, [the Dalai Lama] asked not only whether we knew what [Sharon] was talking about, but also if we ourselves experienced this self-hatred. And almost all the Buddhist teachers there, representing an entire generation, said 'yes.'"

With his hallmark humility, the Dalai Lama responded, "I thought I had a very good acquaintance with the mind, but now I feel quite ignorant. I find this very, very strange."

Some philosophical discussions of this story bring up the point that while it would be hard to say that Tibetan Buddhists and the Dalai Lama have literally never heard of self-hatred or self-aggression, it's simply not emphasized in their spirituality in the way that it is in the western world. Maybe this is because they didn't grow up with the Original Sin soundtrack playing in the background of their lives.

Thrown for a loop, His Holiness wanted to explore the concept of self-hatred further. He was not letting it go. "Is that some kind of nervous disorder?" he asked. "Are people like that very violent?" And then he delivered this white hot Truth in the form of a question:

"But you have Buddha nature. How could you think of yourself that way?"

The trouble with self-Love is…

I'm in Downward-Facing Dog in yoga class when the very bubbly, very young yoga instructor says to us all, "Now when you're down there, just Love yourself." I wanted to punch her. Nice thought, it's even the right thought, but it's just not that simple.

So much of self-help speak is *Love yourself, Love yourself, you gotta Love yourself.* Yes, do! And then the hyper-motivational champs step up to the mic and tell us to *Do what ordinary people fear. Find a way, not an excuse.* Yes, do!

But we're missing the deeper dialogue when it comes to self-Love and determination: Loving yourself, even when you do it most humbly, can attract some not-so-Loving responses. When you start to care more deeply about your own well-being, a whole new set of inner—and outer—challenges will surface in your life. Self-respect can create conflict. Just get used to it.

Slipping out of fullness

You will experience sharp and surprising pangs of self-hatred on your way to self-respect. This is what happens: you're morphing beautifully and certainly into your assured self. You're less critical, more embracing, and, just as marvelously, you are expressing yourself more purely. You're really becoming YOU, through Love. You are Loving yourself into fullness.

And then you slip into the old you for an interminable minute. Something triggers you, and you revert to that former, rougher, or wimpier version of yourself. You try to get something done with your old tricks and tactics—and then you extra extra hate yourself for it.

My journey to Love myself more truly can be summed up in one word: softer. The closer I am to my essence, the softer I become. I'm still fierce, even fiercer in some ways, but I can be on my own edge without being as edgy. More fluid, less angular.

But every once in a while, especially if I'm feeling threatened, my inner Joan Jett takes over. She served me well in high school when I had to be scrappier. And when I was carving out my identity and activist spirit in my early twenties, she was handy. And she was very attractive to dudes who liked a conquest. Joan would jump into my body, and I'd get all rock 'n' roll and respond to any number of issues with this stunningly elegant refrain: "Like I fucking care."

But I grew up. Like, totally. Which is to say, I started to take care of myself in a more well-rounded way. All of myself—my feelings, my body, my money, my future. Turns out, I did fucking care. A lot. I grew into the Truth that I was absolutely, positively worthy of my desires. And I didn't need to scrap or over-compromise to get what I wanted. Instead, radiance and discernment would serve me very, very well. Softer.

Jump to a few months ago: I bumped into a friend in Venice Beach. He's tall, dark, and swoony, and, as luck would have it, my hair was down that day and I was wearing my favourite skirt. We were so happy to see each other, laughing and bright-eyed. In the course of catching up, he asked for my business advice. And then I slipped out of my fullness and into my halfness. I got all masculine and sturdy and started elaborating on the issue. As Brené Brown would put it, I started "hustling for worthiness" as I started channeling Joan Jett for a hot minute. And then I heard myself say it, just in passing about a business issue of my own: "Like I fucking care." I actually spoke it out loud. *Who said that?* 'Cause it wasn't me. It was Joaner. I winced inside. Maybe he didn't even notice, maybe he thought I was as cool as I was trying to be, though I distinctly felt the air ripple with surprise. The conversation naturally flowed to the next topic, with more flirty laughs and a goodbye hug.

That incident plagued me for days. *I can't believe I said that. That's so unlike me. Erase erase. Ewww.* I was ninety-nine percent awesomely myself with Mr. Swoon but that one percent was really irking me. I built a whole therapy session around it. "So why did that one moment of janky inauthenticity hit me so hard?" I asked my psychotherapist, the luminous Anne Davin. "Because the new, more embodied you isn't tolerating the old lies anymore." Ohhhhh. That's *so* why. Word up, Joan Jett. I have moved ON.

> You have to Love the you that you outgrew. These are the disowned parts of yourself that are less spiritually cultivated than you are now. You have to bring them into your heart and treat them like you would a sister or a beloved. Until you reclaim those unintegrated parts of yourself, you do not have your full power— part of you is out there, wandering around, looking for a Loving home or a rock band to belong to.

When you can honour and Love the fool that you used to be, some even greater growth will happen. Stay with me here: you can start to Love the part of you that didn't Love all of you. *You'll give yourself a break for being so self-judgmental.* Then we're *really* talking about self-Love and acceptance.

Fake it to get it

Faking self-Love to get more Love from others...such a clever survival tactic. Fake self-Love might be another way of saying "false pride." We can shout, *I Love my curves! I Love my crazy! I Love my attitude!* All the while, we're looking out of the corner of our eye to see if everyone else is loving us for our curves, our crazy, and our 'tude.

If *I* Love me, then maybe YOU will Love me...right? Not necessarily. Because humans are really messed up about Love. Beautifully, irresistibly, and understandably so messed up about Love.

You can try to Love yourself *in spite of* not being Loved the way you want to be. "You don't dig me? Well, I'll show you how fantastic I am!" And actually, that approach can be somewhat effective, because while you're proving your fabulosity to everyone, you might start seeing and believing it for yourself. But you're still going to have to get past the layers of self-disdain to get to the warm centre of your true adoration, like the Self-Love Tootsie Pop.

Eventually, you must Love yourself just because of, well, your self...your beautiful, luminous, powerful, magnificent, righteous, sacred self.

Signs that you Love yourself

In her warm and plain-speaking way, Buddhist nun Pema Chödrön talks about how many of us spend years taking good care of ourselves with exercise and diet regimes, we get our massages, do our spiritual practices and various forms of meditation, but when we're really challenged by life, we still don't have true self-Love to draw on: "...all those years don't seem to have added up to their inner strength and kindness for themselves that they need to relate with what's happening... When we start to develop unconditional acceptance of ourselves, then we are really taking care of ourselves in a way that pays off." *A way that pays off.*

A way that builds inner strength instead of outer dependencies. A way that expands us so that we can accommodate more pain and more joy. A way that grows us. Deep growth happens when our self-care is a celebration of our goodness and value, and not a fixation on what needs to be fixed. It's a life-affirming attentiveness that steers us inward for the answers. Eventually we stop looking for "signs from the Universe" that we are loved, and we start finding signs—everywhere—that we Love ourselves.

- **You start where you are and Love what you can.**
  Consider that Love, like Truth and Light, exists on a spectrum. On one end, we have hesitant, kind-of Love. On the other end of the scale is free-flowing, certain, pure Love.

  If you want to grow in Love for who you are, you Love what you can on any given day and let that guide you out of the darkness toward bigger, brighter Love. Some days, all you'll be able to muster is Loving the colour of your eyes or how organized you keep your desk. Brilliant. Pick something, anything, to keep your mind off loathing.

  Other days, you'll know with electric certainty that you are a magnificent, connected creature. And that Love affair with your Truth will be your protection, your guide, and your reason for being.

- **You practice good manners with yourself.**
  We self-help overachievers can berate ourselves for our suffering. We say and do things to ourselves that we'd never do to other people. Would you treat anyone else like that? Would you talk to a child like that? Love is patient, Love is kind. Love says, "You poor thing. No wonder you feel this way. It's been tough." Just like your best friend would say after you poured your heart out to her.

You don't need a pep talk or a meditation to distract you. You just need some empathy for yourself.

- **You allow your Light to be reflected back to you.**
When you can't rally some compassion for yourself, then seek it out from your friends and heroes, in a healthy way. That's the beauty of being in this together. We can reflect our lovability to each other. When we're blind to our own Light, someone with open eyes can describe it to us: "But you're amazing, and resourceful, and so kind, and totally hot…"

- **You hang out with people who Love you.**
This isn't elitist or self-help snobbery; it's a minimum health requirement. You grow most vigorously in conditions of kindness, resonance, and good laughter. You don't look at relationships like spiritual boot camp (even though they are). You keep your inner circle full of fellow Love Crusaders (and it only takes one other person to have an inner circle).

- **You prioritize pleasure.**
After years of being hard on ourselves and staying stuck in karmic cycles, pleasure-making is courageous. Pleasure heals. Pleasure makes all of the (seemingly) unavoidable hardships of just. being. here. so much easier. Your pleasure empowers you and you know it.

- **You reward yourself for trying.**
You don't reward yourself *only if* you achieve what you set out to do. And you don't set up consequences if you fail. You commend yourself for showing up because Loving is an unending process, not a finish line.

- **You go beyond "tolerating" your so-called shortcomings to actually accepting more parts of yourself.**
You may think that tolerating your foibles is an achievement in self-compassion, but tolerance is not the same as acceptance.

Tolerance keeps you on guard—you are, effectively, only managing degrees of irritation with yourself. Instead, you accept that, for now anyway, this is what you've got to work with: strengths and weaknesses. Doing this creates an intimacy with yourself that can never be interrupted.

- **You befriend your loneliness.**
The ancient philosopher Plotinus said that on the journey to enlightenment, you go from being alone to Alone. The big Alone is what it feels like to experience yourself as the centre of your Universe. It's a big job. The upside is that this sense of isolation makes us more responsive and available to connect with the world. We care for our loneliness and we care for others, so we care more about what we're creating in the world.

- **You have healthy boundaries.**
You say *Yes* when you mean *Yes*, and *No* when you mean *No*. Because you Love yourself, that's why.

- **You mean what you say.**
Don Miguel Ruiz put it best: "You can measure the impeccability of your word by your level of self-Love. How much you Love yourself and how you feel about yourself are directly proportionate to the quality and integrity of your word." You value your time, you value your word, you Love yourself enough to know that every commitment you make—from the time you say you'll show up, to lifetime vows—is sacred, because you are a sacred being.

- **You take risks.**
How can you be afraid once you've seen the Light of yourself? Expanded with Love, you rise up to meet your quantum self. You see what you're really capable of, and you not only trust yourself more, but you trust that life will back you up when you dare to grow.

- **You apologize.**

  Loving yourself doesn't mean that you think you're right all of the time. When you're so intimate with yourself, you can see exactly where and when you go wrong and hurt other people. You know that your identity won't shatter when you admit to faults. You've got a foundation of self-compassion and awareness to stand on to say, *I'm sorry. I know I can do better, and I will.*

- **You hold out.**

  Holding out is not the same as passive waiting. It's a kind of stamina that springs forth from self-respect. Self-Love gives you the power to say *No, thank you,* to walk away, to be at peace with where things are at—or to accept that you're not at peace but that's okay for now. Self-Love sets all your standards.

- **You Love yourself like it's your job.**

  Loving yourself isn't a luxury or a gift that confident people inherit at birth. Love is the journey *and* the destination. It's how you discern what stays and what goes in your life. Love is the reason you adorn your body and invest in your ideas. Love is your life force, the deciding factor, and your greatest intelligence. Love yourself like your life depends on it—because it does.

- **You will Love more people, more deeply.**

  This is the best part. Self-Love expands into Loving others. It's so perfect, and beautiful, and right. You're not trying to attain your own sequestered happiness. You look into your heart and see that it is connected to everyone else's. You feel that mystical and palpable kinship, and you want the same freedoms and fulfillment for others that you want for yourself.

  Loving and accepting yourself increases your sensitivity to other people's emotional states. You feel other people's pain and yearnings almost as keenly as your own. And you wouldn't have it any other way.

The only guarantee

Here's the white hot Truth: Loving yourself doesn't guarantee that you will be Loved by others.

As a self-celebrating, self-respecting individual, you might really annoy some people. You WILL annoy some people. You will annoy a LOT of people. You will be misunderstood—perhaps thought of as arrogant. You may be uninvited. When you Love yourself enough to say, "This is acceptable in my life and this is not," you will become unacceptable to other people, especially those who tend to push against your boundaries. (You will also become a magnet for real Love and respect, so don't dillydally with the haters.)

Some New Age theories tell us that if we Love ourselves, the world will reflect that state of harmony back to us—because *the world is our mirror*. But it's simply not true. You can own your Love and be met with hatred. That doesn't mean you're not sending the Universe the correct message. It doesn't mean that you're not Loving yourself enough. It means that you're living in a world with other humans who have varying degrees of awareness on their own paths from indifference, to hate, to Love.

The only guaranteed result of Loving yourself is that you will Love yourself.

You're "The One."

Because you said so.

let your preferences evolve

6

YOU'RE SPECIAL— BUT NOT *THAT* SPECIAL

In search of worth

You get your lessons how you get your lessons

I ALWAYS WANTED TO have a near-death experience. But not something too terribly inconvenient or terrifying. I wanted just enough death to get me to the Tunnel of Light. Then, I'd come back with brilliant information for all of humankind. Or a supernatural talent. Like X-ray vision or complete, unwavering faith.

But I've never been struck by lightning. No guru has ever picked me out of the crowd to bless me or give me a Sanskrit name. And I don't see dead people. My enlightenment depends on the machinations of my day-to-day living. Putting on the kettle. My little boy humming, filling the hummingbird feeder. Hungry belly, hungry heart, hungry guy on the corner of 1st & Commercial. Rice with friends. Veins in my heart, tunnels of choices, each leading to the Light every single normal, miraculous day.

Some people get their spiritual lessons delivered in glorious visitations from etheric beings. Some are miraculously healed from their illnesses. Others, a chosen few it would seem, have what Zen Buddhists call a *satori*—a sudden enlightenment experience that renders one illumined, if not a fully realized being.

It's easy to glamourize those spiritual rarities and forget that in many of those cases, those "special" individuals endured massive suffering or extreme circumstances before their breakthroughs. Eckhart Tolle is one such awakened being. Leading up to his enlightenment experience, he was in a long-term, deeply depressive state and contemplating suicide. I think that there are just different tracks of suffering and awakening. Maybe someone like Tolle chose the accelerated program: acute suffering and acute awakening. Others choose the beginner level: suffer moderately over a long time, and gradually awaken.

The danger in wanting to uplift our consciousness is that we might neglect human rootedness. Being multidimensional and yoga-fied seems much cooler than, say, working on your conflict resolution skills in the workplace. Multidimensional IS cool. And so is being right here and being very human.

Special gone wrong: spiritual glamour

> *Half the harm that is done in this world*
> *is due to people who want to feel important.*
> – T.S. Eliot, *The Cocktail Party*

The need to feel special is a healthy human need. It means we're being seen and are loved for what's seen. But when you combine spirituality with an unchecked hunger to be "special," you get spiritual glamour. And it's some nasty, nefarious stuff.

spiritual glamour (noun/verb):

1. regarding your spirituality as a qualification for special treatment; superiority
2. New Age douche

Spiritual glamour–pusses always find a way to insert their esoteric resumé into the conversation. "I've been meditating for twenty-five years," or "My work with the orphans..." or "Parmesan Yogi Wannawanda is a personal friend of mine and when I was yachting with him, he told me..." We get it. You're buds with an Enlightened Master, so you must be special.

Spiritual glamour uses spirituality as shorthand for clout. *I got a download and my Spirit Guides directed me to...* Hey, just because your guides said so doesn't make it more accurate. *I heard in a meditation we're supposed to work together.* Well, that's not what I heard. *I'm "getting" that you should...* I'm getting that you should not give me your opinions masked as esoteric counsel from on high. And, now I have to disagree with you *and* all of your Spirit Guides.

Spiritual glamour sets itself above the people it thinks are less evolved, while simultaneously getting its glitter from those very people's admiration and awe. It also tries very hard to win favour from the Universe by working diligently toward enlightenment. Spiritual glamour thrives on ranking systems and mystical accoutrements. It's very showy. And divisive.

And forgivable.

I think we should all share our mystical stories more freely, if we're inspired to. But it's the *motivation* behind the storytelling that we need to double-check. One person can tell you about their angelic visitation for the sake of connection and being helpful. As a result, their story brings you closer to them—it's unifying.

Another person can tell you that they saw angels or aliens, but the subtext is: *I'm just that much more special than you.* But since they tell you their story in hushed overtones, it's hard to hear the undertones.

When spiritual glamour gets really out of control, it develops into a more dangerous condition: a good old Messiah Complex. While anybody with a conscience feels the suffering of the world around them, those with Messiah Complexes get overly attached to processing other people's suffering. This may sound charitable, but it can be just a part of a campaign for their "bigger vision." Faux Messiahs think they have something extremely unique to offer that will lead to someone's salvation—and they're usually in a big hurry to make it happen. They carry their cross with great pride—and they're reluctant to put it down and join the rest of us working on the ground.

Not very helpful

> The human soul doesn't want to be advised or fixed or saved. It simply wants to be witnessed—to be seen, heard and companioned exactly as it is. When we make that kind of deep bow to the soul of a suffering person, our respect reinforces the soul's healing resources, the only resources that can help the sufferer make it through.
>
> – Parker J. Palmer, *The Gifts of Presence, The Perils of Advice*

I was sorting myself out after a painful breakup and a distant friend wrote to me, along the lines of, "It all makes sense now. Your soul is intact. It's an illusion that you were ever hurt. Nothing exists now but the present. Spirit has given you all you need to evolve."

Evolve THIS, I said as I punched the delete key. This is a quintessential example of disassociation, superiority, and dispassion disguised as spirituality. Someone acts like they want to help, but they can't get off their esoteric high horse to wade through the muck of it beside you. Talk to me like you care about my *feelings*. Relate to me as a human. Like this: "You got hurt. This sucks." That's what enlightenment sounds like when someone is in pain.

Precious

As we spend more time on the spiritual path and our energy frequency literally becomes more refined, we might get more *selective*. About *everything*. Selectivity is badass. It's part of being a deliberate creator. Ideally, our evolving needs don't turn into hyper-sensitivity, the kind that makes ordinary life less tolerable for us and turns us into precious, demanding people.

I'm really clear about what works for me and what doesn't. I like to hang with deep-feeling people, I want clean food prepared with intention, and I don't like heavy metal music in cafés. Except that much of the world is shallow, dirty, and really loud, so if I'm put out when things aren't *just so*, I'm not doing myself or anyone else any favours—I'm just becoming unbearable with what I don't like to bear.

I had a conversation with Reverend Michael Bernard Beckwith about this. "I think we get more specific but more fluid at the same time," I said to him. "You're talking about flexibility and you're talking about unbotherability, which are fruits of the spirit," he said. "There are certain things that one prefers, but if it's not going quite that way, you're not as bothered. You're more available and pliable for that which is trying to happen, to happen. That's a maturity that happens as we evolve." Preferably, we become *unbotherable*.

Sometimes, the most enlightened and loving thing you can do is put up and shut up. Not because you can't speak up for yourself, but because sometimes that's the most graceful option. You eat the meat the hostess serves even though you're a vegetarian. You take the horribly eco-destructive gift and say "Thank you!" You find the common ground in your opposing politics. You apply all your skills of transcendence and you rise above your sometimes-inconvenient principles to embrace what's been brought to you—with Love, even.

We've gotta talk about the ego

The ego. "You gotta become somebody before you can be nobody." This is what most psychologists would say about it. Some contemporary thinkers believe that your ego is an ally on the spiritual path—because the road to wholeness is not for the faint of personality. You'll need the self-assurance and self-interest that the ego provides to carve out your place in the world. **You will need to believe in your innate specialness in order to stand up for yourself.** Which, of course, is not the same as believing that you are more special than anyone else. You're going to rock your unique and everyone else can rock theirs.

Approaches to the ego vary wildly in different spiritual circles, from thinking it should be obliterated and transcended because it's the dictator of all dark behaviours, to respecting it as an integral, and very purposeful part of our human makeup. The range of ego opinions leaves a lot of room for confusion to happen—and more self-denigration on the self-help path. Possessing an ego has become one more reason to be down on yourself.

Saint John Cassian, a Christian monk and theologian from the 4th century, was on the extreme side of the ego argument: "Every task, every activity, gives this malicious demon a chance for battle." Not so good. Much more middle-of-the-road was Zen philosopher Alan Watts: "The ego is a dithering of consciousness which is the same as anxiety." So then, the ego *is* part of being conscious, just not part of being *highly* conscious.

Eckhart Tolle teaches extensively about the egoic self and the ego's critical need to maintain a sense of separateness—or specialness—in order to survive. But he also says, "If you consider the ego to be your personal problem, that's just more ego." Jungian psychologist Marion Woodman declared that trying to rid oneself of the ego "rapes the soul." I'm with her. The ego is part of the human package. Trying to vanquish it is not only impossible, but the attempt itself is destructive.

Misplaced blame

Because self-helpers are so well-versed in the perils of excessive ego, we can be overly diligent about reining it in. **We can even mislabel some of our best qualities as the work of the ego.**

I had a business partner who often admonished me for moving "too fast." I did have the need for speed. I loved the smell of a product launch in the morning. I wanted to break even in eighteen months instead of three years. I was always looking for the most direct route from A to B. And after a number of confrontations between her belief that I moved too quickly and my belief that she moved too slowly, I got downhearted on myself and concluded that it must be my lusty ego (that malicious demon!) that was spurring me on.

But hells no, it was the holy entrepreneurial spirit. When I finally went solo, it became clear that my knack for velocity is one of my most heart-sourced talents. I had been using the ego label as an excuse to dim my Light. I was too willing to relegate my genuine specialness in order to be more "spiritual."

Putting it in its place

This being human is a guest house.
Every morning a new arrival.
A joy, a depression, a meanness,
some momentary awareness comes
as an unexpected visitor.
Welcome and entertain them all!
– Rumi

Befriending our ego is a step to befriending our whole self. Think of the fear-mind, the ego, as the monster at your table. It's your monster. It's your creation and you're going to treat it like part of the family, because it is. And like most of your family, your inner creature responds quite well to Love and clear expectations. *Hey, I see you. I know you have something* *to tell me. I'm so glad you told me that. I'm so glad you showed me why I'm frightened. And since you're at my table now, please sit up and use your utensils.* If you try to banish your ego monster, it will just break through the windows to get back in. With some effort, you'll see that it wasn't necessarily misbehaving. It was just trying to make you feel special.

You're an original

If we're always looking to see how "spiritual" others think we are, we will never tap the depths of our authentic selves. Their perceived opinions of us will be the greatest distractions from hearing and feeling our Truth. The desire to evolve must come from internal inspiration, not external motivation.

There are healthy and unhealthy ways to relate to our ego. If we think we're not secure or high enough on some spiritual hierarchy, we're likely to use our ego in some ugly ways to try to advance. We'll try to overcome or silence our ego by becoming hyper-spiritual, which of course is a total trap that keeps us from getting our needs for communion met—with ourselves and with Life.

> **Wanting to be spiritually admired is very different from being spiritually admirable. You're the only one who can validate your spiritual integrity.**

I was at a spiritual retreat in the Catskill Mountains. The Brahma Kumaris, one of my favourite organized faiths, had brought together a group of activists, UN officials, and progressive business and political types to talk about vocational calling and social service. I was there because I was running a think-tank in Washington, D.C. at the time.

On the opening night, about forty of us sat in a circle of plushy chairs. The facilitator asked us to introduce ourselves. "Hello, my name is Robert So-and-So," began the elegant gentleman next to me. Then, inspired, he added, "And my spiritual name is Walking Bear." Cool. That sparked a full spiritual name disclosure by everyone else that followed. "Hi, my name is Madeline. My spiritual name is Bindu; it means 'point of light.'" Awesome. "Hello everyone, my name is Christopher. My spiritual name is Ananda. It was given to me by Satchitananda and it means 'bliss.'" Great...but this was getting bizarre. Everyone in the room, dignitaries and all, seemed to have been bestowed a spiritual name. "I'm Lisa, my spiritual name is Shanti." "Kurt here, my guru named me Satya." I was feeling behind the eight ball as the introductions reached me, the last person in the circle to speak. I thought about using the porn name formula: your first pet's name plus the street you grew up on, which would have made me Jessie Maidstone. I opted for the facts.

I said, "Hellooo...my name is Danielle LaPorte, and my spiritual name is...Danielle LaPorte." In between everyone's laughter, I added, "My mother gave it to me." Comedic pause. "She thinks it's special. And so do I."

Work with what you're given. That kind of full acceptance is the most spiritual act of all.

fall madly
in love
with your
humanity

7
SUPER. HUMAN.
Choosing to really be here

Normal amazing

I have not known Shams or oil wells in my living room.
No inheritance, nor near-death experiences.
My blood is mixed
and I am broke in some places.

I have so much confusion I can't find words.
Things to be ashamed of? Or light houses on my way?
Honestly, I can't tell you the difference.

But I walk up a street everyday. The same street. Uphill.
I have a house on this street that I paid for with useful ideas.
In the front yard there is buried a Hummingbird
that I found on the city curb
where I parked my car
on the way to dinner
with a friend who loves me.
I wrapped it up in a cocktail napkin and drove it home.

The bird reminds me that Joy is worth dying for.
And that in my house there is so very much to worship:
A world of Light and determination in the form of a boy with
my smile—

makes me wonder why I ever want more than what I've got:
a Universe on a sidewalk,
an empire of generous questions,
a life that Hummingbirds and the homeless can feast upon.

Resisting my humanity

There is in us an instinct for newness, for renewal, for a liberation
of creative power. We seek to awaken in ourselves a force which really
changes our lives from within. And yet the same instinct tells us
that this change is a recovery of that which is deepest, most original,
most personal in ourselves. To be born again is not to become
somebody else, but to become ourselves.

– Thomas Merton, *Love and Living*

IN MY TWENTIES, I was fascinated by stories of spiritual transcendence. A temple librarian in India told me about a monk in the mountains of Tibet who sat in perpetual meditation (no food, no water, no interaction) for three solid years. He was so far gone—inwardly—that when he emerged, he found that birds had nested on his head and ants had eaten away his earlobes. *That's* focus. I loved hearing about breatharians, individuals who, with the bolstering of meditative practice, subsist on minimal liquids and just...air. Yep. And wandering yogis, and out-of-body experiences, and astral travel, and...

"This is my last lifetime here," I declared to a girlfriend while we hennaed our hands, Nag Champa incense and the Cocteau Twins wafting through the air. "I'm burning some karma, then I'm outta here." I planned to assign myself to another dimension in the next life, ideally one that didn't have melancholy or menstrual cramps. I wanted all Light, all the time.

I'd never felt one hundred percent committed to life on Earth. I'd always planned on seeing this lifetime through, with flair, but I felt like this dimension was just a training ground to get me to higher ground.

Then a miracle of all human miracles happened when I was 34: my son was born. The intensity of our connection—it was like a wave of Light washing away all of my human hesitancies. It was so much of what I needed to realize in one place. *So this is what it's all about.* This *is what the human trip is really for.* This *is what we're made of. Pure Love.* And there I was—here—and I didn't want to be anywhere else.

Now, that didn't stop me from wanting to earn my keep, from thinking I needed to work harder to earn my pleasure and ensure my wellness. On the contrary: I was going to try even harder to be superhuman, not just for me, or for God, but for my boy.

Compared to whom?

I once asked a meditation instructor how he thought people with full-time jobs and children at home were ever going to get enlightened with such packed schedules. "'Cause this is some time-consuming stuff," I told him. "Householders," he replied. "There's room for Householders." This means laypeople, the non-monastics—they are free to be out and about in the world, have families, watch reality TV. The melting distinction between monastics and laities is considered to be a sign of progress for Buddhism in the West. Flexibility for the win.

Many spiritual practices cultivate the capacity to rise above the illusions of the mind, to reach our higher self so we can get perspective on our smaller self. To witness Truth. And, to be sure, the power of observation is the benefit of devoted practice.

All of my research into ascetics and contemplatives had me thinking that ascension was The Great Spiritual Aim. That if I wasn't developing a super-consciousness, I was too ordinary, too *human*. Out of touch. And worse, out of favour with the invisible cosmic crew I was always trying to earn points with.

I do believe that *upward* is where we want to be heading—toward a higher point of view. I want to transcend my fears, ascend to unity, rise above the mundane. But I have to take the mundane with me on my way to the holy. Otherwise, I am not whole. Otherwise, I am leaving God behind.

My religious investigations were accruing. The sādhus! What a fascinating, freaky show of devotion they are. Known as India's holy men, these ascetic Hindus offer up their entire existence to prayer and pilgrimage, live off the alms of the community, and are dreadlocked, body-painted, and barely clothed. In some sects, as acts of physical transcendence, they hang bricks off of their pierced penises. Hardcore. This had me question my pain tolerance. I heard about modern Christian monks who regularly self-flagellate with a "passion stick" as a means of subduing temptation. And other Orthodox Christian brothers who stood or kneeled in prayer on high rock outcroppings for years, until they became crippled. And there I was, shopping for the softest yoga mat I could find to support my practice.

A bunch of friends were doing vipassana retreats and I was feeling like a total underachiever because I had zero interest in sitting on a cushion for ten days watching my in-breath and out-breath. *What am I afraid of? I must be overly attached to my un-awakeness.* Between all my strict vegan besties and my friend who gave up sugar for a whole year (not. even. ketchup. How can you live a fulfilling life without ketchup?), I felt guilty every time I opened the fridge. If I didn't turn my weekly walks around my neighbourhood lake into a walking meditation, as per Thích Nhất Hạnh, I felt like a slacker. If I wasn't chanting in the car, I felt like I wasn't making the most of my drive time. A lama I was working with gave me the assignment to chant one hundred thousand prajnaparamita mantras. A friend of mine who was also practicing with the same teacher said, "Oh is that all? You can bang those out in a weekend!" Bang out mantras? That was a new one for me.

Within the same week my phone notified me of five apps to track my mindfulness. That was it—I was maxed. I couldn't count another step or mantra. I needed a Super Woo quantification break.

Ancient. Modern. Monks. Neighbours.

Torturing ourselves to ascend.

I understand how renouncing the ego and bodily form could be very useful in attaining enlightenment—to truly experience that we are more than what our senses see and feel. To let go of desirous fixations, to master one's consciousness by transcending the biological locality—that which we call a "body"—of our spirit, *this* is mastery. And I suspect I've lived lifetimes whipping my own back and blistering my knees to feel the ecstasy of subsuming pain and offering it up to a higher power.

Perhaps in my next go-round I'll be born into a lineage of high-level practitioners and devote myself to an ascetic life willingly and with fervor. Maybe before this life of mine is over, when I'm silvery and shrunken and my lover has gone into the Light ahead of me, I'll find a cabin in the woods and sit in repose to transmute every breath into Light for the Multiverse. Maybe.

But here's where I am now: I will not, in any way, torture myself to ascend. Not even if there's an app for it. The hours I've logged in lotus position have indeed expanded my mind. All the Light I've been trained to bring down and radiate outward has kept me well, and maybe it's even helped some others. And maybe I am clinging to this theory because it's a comforting one, but I'm convinced that there is a more joyful route to Soul expansion. It's not easy, and it's not fast, but it involves as much pleasure as it does restraint. I'm working on being a super human, not superhuman.

What I know in my bones is that for most of us, our greatest growth comes from the black mucky fertile mess of relationships, when you do the hard work of loving someone the way they deserve to be loved. When you go down into the sensuality of the present. When you go down into surprising self-hatred, into feeling helpless in the midst of ignorance and toxins and homelessness. When you show up to help yourself and help others.

My life always calls me, sometimes wrenches me, back down to my body, my home, like a million other homes on Earth, filled with minutiae and temperaments and soft tiny experiences of joy and pain.

...

That baby boy of mine grew into a strong swimmer, but he flunked one of his swim classes before passing the program. Total bummer. As I was handing him a towel at the community centre pool, I said, *Just breathe in Light. What colour of Light do you need?* "Mom, you praying about green Light isn't making me feel any better," he said, obviously flustered by my methods. "Please just get my backpack and let's go home." Got it.

After years of wanting to ascend, I'm just really grateful to be here. I hope you can say the same.

protect your
heart so
you can
keep it
wide open

8

OPEN, GENTLE HEART. BIG FUCKING FENCE.
Boundaries for spiritual people

The tolerance trap

W E DO IT for Love, we do it to feel in control, we do it because we think it's a moral responsibility: whatever the reason, we take a lot of shit in the name of being spiritual. Specifically, we become more and more...and more and more...*tolerant.*

I'm all for the kind of tolerance that happens when your heart is so big that you can give ample space to opinions that differ from yours. *You be you, I'll be me, maybe we can meet in the middle for green juice and a beer.* That type of tolerance is deliciously sophisticated.

And you *know* I'm all for unbridled Love. The golden-intersection-of-heaven-and-earth kind of Love. White hot and steady. *That* kind of Love—for self and others. (Which is rare, often comes with a series of initiations, and is worth holding out for, by the way.)

But when we combine a sense of unworthiness with the aspiration for self-improvement, we can become *overly* tolerant. We take a lot of guff because we don't believe that we deserve better—but we're trying hard to be better so we can earn better treatment. Translation: **insane loyalty, foolish compassion, excessive tolerance.**

When we're painfully aware of our own imperfections, we might think, "How dare I expect someone else not to have imperfections?" We end up prolonging our involved suffering because we think that whoever we're trying to heal, or train to treat us better, is also coming from a wounded place—and that it's our spiritual j-o-b to be in "the process" together.

If only I were more Loving, they would…

> *Spirituality is not some pale-pink, gauzy, psychologically unsophisticated understanding of the world. Rather, it represents the most profound elucidation of how the mind operates and how it filters our experience. It recognizes the extraordinary depth of our most fundamental yearning—our yearning for love— and the extraordinary pain that we feel when we don't find it.*
>
> – Marianne Williamson, *Tears to Triumph*

A good friend of mine was married to a bit of a chump. Let's call them Sasha and…Dick. Dick was a massage therapist. One day, he shared with Sasha that one of his patients had explicitly invited him to have an affair— which he politely declined. Sasha, being the regular meditator that she was, was super chill. "Fidelity is so hot, babe," she congratulated her man. "So what did she say when you told her you couldn't treat her anymore?" As Sasha explained to me, Dick "got that angry shame-face combo that he does." Because, he'd already booked her for another treatment. Sasha then said, pointedly, "You're not going to rub her naked body every week now that she's put the moves on you…*right?*"

Three couples therapy sessions later, Dick reluctantly agreed to *consider* letting this client go. Sasha and I were having one of our regular multitasking morning calls while making our smoothies. "Am I being a demanding freak?" she asks me. "Maybe I should just try to lean into this and be more trusting, like Dick says."

"This isn't about you being a crazy, jealous lady—which you're not," I said. "This is about really basic respect. He should have shut this shit down the first time the chick propositioned him."

"Ya." Sasha said, and paused. "But he's just coming from that place where he's all wounded and then gets all stubborn." Sigh. "I get it. Hurt dogs bite." I said. Then, "Okay, loud noise." Which is where we both mute our phones and turn on our blenders.

Sasha plowed through dozens of relationship how-to books and worked herself into an over-analyzing frenzy about the principles of unconditional Love, relationships being your mirrors, and how the divine feminine is supposed to give the divine masculine more "space."

Meanwhile, many couples therapy sessions later, Dick still hadn't stopped greasing up the potential adulteress—in a professional capacity, *of course*—on a weekly basis.

The relationship was doomed for many reasons. After Sasha and the Dickster eventually split (alleluia), a bunch of us girls were in my living room. One of the new girls in our circle asked, "So why'd you stay with him for so long?" Sasha sighed. "I thought I could Love him into changing. My loyalty was, like, *insane*." Truth.

More Truth: it's not just guys like Dick who take advantage of tolerant partners. It's a two-way street. Many of us growth-oriented individuals use what we call "Love" as a form of power to try to get people to conform to meet our needs. *I Love you so I see you. I'm rooting for you and I can help you. Just let me help you.* Subtext: *I'm more knowing, and you need to change. Please change.* And maybe "they" do need to change—desperately and as clear as day.

But if we're operating from our real power, rooted in our self-Love and respect, we'd steer clear of people who obviously aren't going to meet our most important needs. We would avoid taking on relationships as "projects" and instead seek relationships centred around growing together. We'd get with people who see us as clearly as we see them—and we'd co-write a true Love story in that beautiful Light.

We've got to talk about narcissism

Let's say that your commitment to lovingkindness is getting you somewhere deeper, brighter, truer. You're incredibly receptive and understanding. Being on the spiritual path has cultivated greater empathy within you. It's amazing.

You know who can sniff out empathetic people like bloodhounds? Highly narcissistic people. You'd think that because empathetic people, particularly women, are more in tune with energy and our own feelings, that we'd know immediately when someone else has jacked into our life force and is sucking on it *hard*. But, since we're committed to the journey and all, we just keep tolerating it.

Now, let's bear in mind that we all have some degree of self-centredness at play. This should ensure that we don't run wild, labelling everyone as a narcissist. Just because your partner wants more room in the closet or you don't agree on movie selections, or your boss wants people to pronounce their name properly, does not mean they need to seek immediate counselling. So...*perspective*. With so much Psych 101 material available to us, we may be throwing around diagnoses a little too freely. It's like, totally *borderline sociopathic*.

I'm bringing this up because bona fide, high-level narcissism seems to be having its way with people who are sincerely trying to generate more Light in their lives.

From what I gather, Jung saw narcissism as a continuum from health to sickness and didn't discriminate against narcissism—it's as legitimate a choice as any. He also believed that to be psychologically healthy, we have to strike a balance between the demands of society and what we really are. Heinz Kohut, an American psychoanalyst, was one of the first important people in the field to talk about healthy narcissism. He believed that if early "normal" narcissistic needs were adequately met (to be validated, respected, positively differentiated) a person would then grow into a "mature form of positive self-esteem; self-confidence"—a.k.a. healthy narcissism.

I'd define healthy narcissism as, "I'm all about me, *and!* I can be all about you! In fact, I take great pleasure in being both." You feel GREAT about who you are most of the time. And you want other people to feel just as great about themselves. Healthy narcissism helps you feel self-assured but also realistic. So, your confidence doesn't get in the way of genuine connection and intimacy, and your self-interest doesn't become a superiority complex. Healthy.

Full tilt, *unhealthy* narcissism is all about itself. Period. *Me, me, me, and even though it may not look like it…I make sure it all gets back to me, me, and by the way…me.*

You can say a lot of negative things about narcissism, but the truest one is that underneath it all, narcissists feel insecure and inadequate. They do NOT feel great about themselves most of the time. Narcissism is a disease of feeling less-than.

An unhealthy narcissist has a hard time seeing other points of view because that might mean that theirs is wrong—so they will go to great lengths to be right (they are masters of the blame game). Narcissists suck at real intimacy because they do not want to be seen or worse, shamed for what is seen. They can use charm as a survival tactic. They tend to create unrealistic plans and grandiose goals because it makes them feel bigger. They can't really lose themselves in Love because they are clutching so tightly to their own identity. They're extremely defensive because they are fighting for their life. Narcissists have turned their backs to their Souls and they're looking for a Light source from other people.

Those are legitimate reasons to feel compassion for high-spectrum narcissists—compassion is a brilliant response to all pain. But don't get too soft. Because this is where bright, spiritually inclined people (read: a lot of New Age women) become the "perfect pairing" for this mismatch. Narcissists are driven to fill the holes in their Souls. And who better to recruit for the job than Soul-full people?

Not everyone is your mirror, okay?

One thing that the self-help movement loves to teach and re-teach is that we attract certain people into our lives to teach us certain things. I'm down with that theory. One hundred percent.

But there's a derivative concept that gets dangerous: that we manifest people because they are, on some level, a reflection of ourselves. If you buy this, then you would have to conclude that if you attract a narcissist into your life, or just any really selfish person, then, on some level, you're just like them.

I'll put this as poetically I can: just because you've brought a total jerk-face into your reality, it doesn't mean that they are mirroring your inner jerkface-ness. It might just mean that they're a total jerk. And you're not. And the only thing you need to "work on" is how you deal with them.

Since, cosmically speaking, we are all "one," then everything is indeed a reflection of everything else. If you want to drill into the depths of your personhood to find your own shadowy bits that are vaguely similar to the jerk who's giving you a hard time—have at it. Searching for reflection and connection is a very spiritually responsible approach. But don't take that shred of evidence and turn it into a case against yourself.

Sometimes, they're just a jerk. It's precisely that karmic—and that great of an opportunity. That a jerk might have come into our lives not so that we can hear our own faults echoing back at us, but to get us to face the fact that for X number of years, we've had a bizarre agreement that it's somehow our job to fix other people. It's an opportunity to burn old contracts and to know how you *don't* want to feel—which is excellent intel for knowing how you *do* want to feel. It's an occasion to look in the mirror and reclaim the power staring back at you.

Boundaries: fences that support your freedom

In all my efforts to Love more more more for change change change, it never actually occurred to me to protect my most powerful asset: my own heart. I thought that giving it away, without much discretion, would get me what I wanted more quickly: communion, connection, *fun*.

I equated "being protective" with "being closed down." I thought if I didn't befriend everyone, I'd be cutting off *the flow of spirit*. I thought if I wanted reciprocity, then I wasn't really giving freely. I thought that if I made myself inaccessible to certain people or situations, then all of the good stuff in life wouldn't be able to access me.

It was too much *flow* and not enough restraint. I was a river in need of some riverbanks. I overpaid people, because Love is generous. I let shoddy behaviour slide, because Love is forgiving. I put off getting a lawyer, because Love is reasonable.

I understood, conceptually, that I am Love itself, as we all are. I am generous, and forgiving, and reasonable—to the core. And if I had to be something other than that, something, say, more stern and delineating, it took some mustering. It wasn't until I let myself be taken advantage of in a series of relationships and was forced to withdraw my Love that I realized how necessary that sacred restraint was.

As I built the necessary walls, I felt like I was annihilating myself, brick by brick, as if I might disappear in the new configuration of "you stay on that side, and I'll stay on this side." I was so unused to having "sides" at all. It truly felt like I was going to die a slow death if I stopped giving so freely, even if that giving was hurting me.

I saw this with my Soul sisters as well. Otherwise remarkably powerful, get-shit-done women who couldn't tell their adorable but free-loading brother that it was time to move out of their guest room and get a job; or the gorgeous and articulate friend who kept quiet about the Tantra teacher who crossed the line with her; or the whip-smart entrepreneur who couldn't put a "stop payment" on the cheque to the "socially responsible" consultant who gave her nearly fatal business advice. We were all so accustomed to directing our compassion outward that turning the tide of protective Love toward ourselves was discombobulating. We fought for causes, for relationships, for our children, for our co-workers, but it was terrifying to fight for ourselves.

The new behaviours required of me felt foreign, even as I knew I needed them. It was a gradual, sometimes rough learning curve. My hands shook the day I sent the text that said, "Perhaps I haven't been clear. Please stay off my property." In other instances, I fretted about team morale, but I curbed my inclinations to give everyone a raise every time we crossed a finish line. In the middle of an uncomfortable misunderstanding with a colleague, I did something radically new: I didn't rush to make them feel better. Their mind was made up, so I let them believe I was to blame and I got on with my work—because it was the most compassionate action to take for myself.

The mid–20th century mystic Gurdjieff said that "we are all idiots of one kind or another." Gotta love a straight-talking mystic. His long list of human follies included "the compassionate idiot." Chögyam Trungpa, a Buddhist meditation master who rose to popularity in the '80s, is also said to have coined the term "idiot compassion." As an act of, ahem, compassion, I'm going with "foolish compassion" to sum this up.

Because, I don't think we're idiots, per se, for trying to get what we need on both primal and mature levels. We're wired to strive for Love. Feminine creatures are particularly inclined to give of themselves as life support. We bleed quite willingly because that's what you do when people you care about so deeply are emotionally anemic or have been injured by life—you give them your blood and your Love. *Here, take some of mine. I can always make more.*

It's crucial to know that foolish compassion is a cousin of the psychotherapy concept of "enabling." We don't want to see someone else suffering, and at the same time, we want to get our needs met or avoid the pain of the situation altogether, so we give in and endure—and we call it compassion. But not only do we hurt ourselves by tolerating demeaning treatment or aggression, we also feed the other person's monster. Being compassionate of yourself by not accepting poor behaviour offers the other person involved the opportunity to look at themselves. It's their choice to use that information to get closer to their Soul, or not.

Fool for Love...foolish compassion...the remedy for both is the same: the courage to hold true to your ideals in real Love, and then to give your full loyalty, your wisest compassion, and your most gracious tolerance—to everyone who meets you where you are.

I'm a Lover. Can't stop, won't stop. And that being the case, my heart deserves safe-guarding. This divine paradox saved my life:

Protect your heart so that you can keep it wide open.

My number one mission with my kid, other than keeping him away from bad drugs and predators, is to assist him in keeping his heart open and expressive. If I can help him cultivate fierce tenderness, he will always be in touch with his power. Here's what I've been saying to him since he was about ten. Now, it's a favourite old story that we love to tell, a story that loves to be told:

"FEEL EVERYTHING. Keep your heart open, as wide open as you can. Open, open, open. Sooo soft.

"And then...put a big fucking fence around it.

"Make the fence tall and make it strong. Ask your angels to guard the gate at all times. Do not let anybody past your gate unless you think that they *also* have an open, gentle heart. Only let in people who are respectful, and interested, and really really loving. Emphasis on respectful."

"Got it, dude?" I say to him.

"Got it!" he confirms. "Mom, can I say what you said, about the fence?"

"You mean the swearing part?" I ask.

"Yeah!"

"Only if you say the 'open, gentle' part first. And then don't repeat this at school."

"Open, gentle heart. Big fucking fence!"

'Atta boy.

The good, hard work

Setting boundaries is challenging for most people. It's especially challenging for holistically inclined women, because we tend to want to merge and connect—with everything. For some of us, learning to set healthy boundaries will be the undertaking of our lifetime, the ultimate work of self-reverence.

One of my favourite wisdom-keepers and coaches, Lianne Raymond, has a great take on it: "I think of boundaries as being the natural outcome of a person who has grown into a mature, actualized being. Imagine coming to the edge of a river. If the river is full and flowing as you stand there on the riverbank, you are going to think twice about crossing it. The flowing presence is in itself a natural boundary. Now imagine that the same river has dried right up, the riverbed is dry and walkable—you might walk across without even hesitating.

"It is the same with people. When they are present and full of themselves in the best possible way, there is no question of invading them, crossing them, or walking over them."

We're easy to invade when we aren't flowing with our own fullness.

At some point in your life, erecting boundaries between you and others might feel like the most trying, demanding, gut-wrenching, impossible work that you've ever been forced to do. You might worry about being cut out of the will, or kept from your dreams, or that lies are circulated about you—by the people on the other side of your boundaries. They will hurl "I *knew* it!" projections at you: "I *knew* you were cold. I *knew* you were flighty. I *knew* you were capable of this." Yes, yes I *am* capable of this—this marvelous thing called *having standards*.

Boundary overkill

> *Boundaries are not walls. They are a living container within which your desires can breathe, gestate and grow until they are ready to be born.*
> – Hiro Boga

Boundaries aren't the same as barriers. Whereas boundaries are proactively on the offence, barriers are hyperactively on the defense.

Think of it this way: boundaries are like a fence with a gate—the energy can come and go and you have space to roam freely and privately behind the fence. You can make it a white picket fence or something more...

electric. It's your fence. The point is you feel safe, and therefore experience more peace.

Barriers are like a heavy shield that you have to drag around with you all of the time, ready to defend yourself from frontal attacks, but leaving the rest of yourself unprotected. It's not very peaceful. Being on guard all the time is anxiety-inducing. You expend your energy fighting off a strike, then you wait for the next attack, hoping it doesn't happen. You can't relax in that position. You're still focused entirely on whatever you're trying to protect yourself from.

Upholding boundaries takes some practice. You might go a bit over-board until you get the hang of it. You put locks on the doors and get a guard dog when all you had to do was say, "I need to cancel lunch." You might quit the committee when all you needed to do was Skype into meetings instead of making the long commute. Or maybe your first iteration of boundaries is way too flimsy (hopefulness is a hard habit to break)—and you realize that you're maxed out and need to clear your calendar for twelve months. And get a guard dog.

Your boundaries might indeed hurt someone. You may offend some-one. You may break someone's heart, and your heart will break for them. You will—and this is very counter to the general New Age vibe—create disharmony. But when you let people take advantage of you, when you ignore the mismatch between their actions and their words, when you let someone call you things that you are not, you are disrespecting your Truth. *That* is the ultimate disharmony. And no true good can come of it.

Because your boundaries protect your well-being and joy, you will have more Love—and patience and understanding to give when you choose. When you're present, you'll be really present. When you give your *Yes*, you'll give it all the way. You're not emotionally shut down. You're emo-tionally clear—crystal clear.

When you respect your valuable time, when you listen to what your body tells you, when you create space for peace in your life—you are in harmony with your Soul. From that equilibrium, you can create master-pieces, you can weather life's storms, and you can help heal a lot of people, starting with yourself.

You want to be ethical, Loving, and harmonious? Respect your ideals. Look up to yourself. Raise your standards for Love, and the Universe will meet you there.

"All is forgiven" includes you.

9

READY TO FORGIVE

The complicated, gritty path to grace

If your compassion does not include yourself, it is incomplete.
– Jack Kornfield, *Buddha's Little Instruction Book*

IT'S COMPLEX. IT'S confusing. It's deeply particular. It's the through-line of most mystical teachings:

Forgiveness.

I'm a "Forgiveness Aspirant." I'm just as good at holding a grudge as I am at letting it go, but for the most part, I want to be as gracious as possible, and I really do believe that forgiveness is the primary Light source of an illumined existence.

That said, choosing—at a critical moment—*not to forgive* was one of the most spiritual, Soul-affirming acts of my life.

For me, divorce was like having my bones broken very, very slowly, one limb after the next, and then each rib—which made it difficult to breathe for a long time. It was brutal. It didn't matter that I was the one walking away. I had to crawl my way back into the Light. The dismantling of the marriage agreement itself was very civilized and straightforward. But I had no idea that the real work had just begun. You can't move on to a new life until you unpack the old one—or burn it down to the ground.

So, I unpacked. I also torched, and past-life-regressed, and journaled, and therapized, and danced, and raged, and grieved, and owned my way through every inch of the journey. I had to go back and do some of it over again, just to make sure it was out of my system. I was not going to take the past into my future. I held up each memory and emotion to surmise: is this a Truth or is this a lie? I was extremely thorough. And when my work was done, which took way longer than I would have preferred, I had become one of those rebirthed, empowered woman clichés. All I could say when asked was, "I'm better than ever. Like, *better than ever.*"

Toward the end of that long trip, I was working with an exquisite healer—she's a total energy ninja. We were working on getting my adrenals back in shape. Cutting some energy cords, putting some astral protection into place...you know, the usual. I'd had a series of disturbing dreams that week, indicators of "intrusions," you could say. I was ready to analyze them, up my frankincense oil intake, chant some Durga mantras, and keep on keeping on.

At the end of a text exchange we were having about the effects of Light meditation on the nervous system, this Lady Ninja of the Light wrote, "D, you have to forgive him." My face flushed with heat and my stomach sank. It wasn't what I was expecting to hear. I'd come so far. My life was beginning to shimmer. My money was mine, I was back in my body, my heart was lush with Love and gratitude. So much of my reinvention had been about reckoning and validating my sanity for all the times that I'd thought I was crazy. I was finally seeing clearly. I had boundaries in place. I was over it.

I read that sentence over three times. "D, you have to forgive him." Then I burst into hot, panicked tears. I'd been calm just moments before. Now I was frantic. Because here's what I heard echoing inside of the words "forgive him":

"Dismantle your boundaries, make yourself wrong, admit to things you never did so everyone thinks you're nicer and saner than you may appear, let him back into your heart, and effectively dissolve your last few years of intense self-scrutiny and resurrection. And while you're at it, let him into your house, be friendly, be a progressive family unit, and for God's sake, smile more—because that is what it means to be a truly spiritual person, Danielle."

At least that's how I interpreted it.

My phone rang. (Lady Ninja of the Light is so tuned in that she could feel my panic across the country.) I didn't bother to compose myself before I answered. I just received the call and wept into the phone.

Let me pause here and say that this ninja healer is one of the most cherished beings in my life. When I figure out one of the esoteric riddles she gives me, I feel accomplished. I want to continue learning from her as long as I can. Her respect matters to me—a lot.

She listened gently on the other end of the line as I cried and cried.

After a minute or so, she said, "D?"

I felt like I was in a movie version of an ancient Greek myth. I was the sweaty protagonist, sword in hand, tired as hell, trying to stay alive in a succession of tests. Do I go left down the maze, or right? Do I scale the wall, or do I accept defeat?

I took a stuttered but full inhale because in that moment, I knew which way I was going to go. I also knew that my beloved mentor would see me as an unfit spiritual student, and our time together would come to an end.

"I'm sorry," I broke the silence. "But I just can't do it." Long pause. "I can't forgive if it means letting him back into my heart. I've come too far." Silence. What I was thinking was, *I know you think I'm a loser, but I really have no choice. Thank you for working with me; you can break up with me now.*

I wanted to be spiritually respectable, but I just couldn't care about "evolving" anymore. For once, I was only exactly where I was. No aspiration, all acceptance. My knowing was coursing through my body; it felt impossibly wrong to abandon it. So there I stood, with my inconvenient Truth. I don't think I've ever been as human as I was in that moment.

And then Lady Light burst out laughing her *oh, honey-child* kind of laugh. "Oh, God no! You do not have to give him the time of day. Ever again. Noooo. Just forgive his SOUL!" She laughed some more. "It's actually the hardest work to do—because that's what's real."

"So don't let down my guard?" I said, all snuffly and hopeful.

"Nope. Please don't."

"Forgive his Soul?" I confirmed.

"Yep. The biggest thing there is."

"Oh! Well I can do THAT! I'm halfway there!"

"You're *way more* than halfway there. This is the finish line," she affirmed.

"Well, that's all you needed to say!" Then we laughed that awesome post-sobbing, post-skill-testing-question, full-bodied woman laugh. Sweet relief! I was going to stay the course:

Keep it real, aim high, do the divine work.

Of course, it wasn't quite that easy—the actual forgiveness practice of my Soul addressing his was profoundly painful at times. But it didn't last long. At that stage, it was like removing slivers instead of cracking bones.

I sat in meditation, and over the course of many months, I streamed Light and Love to his Higher Self. I pictured him standing directly in front of me and I gazed at him with total kindness. If that felt too close for comfort on that day, then I'd just imagine him as a Light form of pure energy. I allowed his Soul to come near to mine again. I let myself adore who he *truly* is. And I thanked him, over and over again, for participating in our agreement to play out what we did in this lifetime. I took it a step further and extended the same gratitude to all of the people in his life. I prayed for their well-being. I cherished his very Soul. Completely.

By honouring my humanity, I got fuller access to my divine power. On Earth, in the day-to-day, my boundaries stayed very much intact. And I moved forward much more freely, navigating with a lighter heart.

Not the goal

Although we know that forgiveness is an experience *of the spirit*, we might be tempted to yank it down from the ethers and hammer it into a goal with a due date—make it an achievable task, get it over and done with. But forgiveness is usually an organic and utterly inefficient process. You can't leap from hurt to clarity, or from anger to absolution. You have to walk there, one revelatory, resentful, intentional step at a time.

Forced or feigned forgiveness can derail the healing process. When we fake-forgive someone, the camouflaged hurt will unearth itself eventually. And by then, it's been festering and there's an even bigger mess to clean up. Seething resentment, dragging up the past, blowing a fuse because your partner said that precise thing that clearly indicates that they haven't changed in the least since you last reamed them out for not changing.

Instead of spouting New Age jargon about how *everything happens for a reason* or that *karma had a hand in things*, it might be more reasonable (a.k.a. human) to just straight-up admit it: "I'm not ready to forgive yet."

This may not go over so well in your Power of Positive Thinking Mastermind Group who take issue with your personal stand on "forgiving when I am damn well ready to forgive." They'll sweetly tell you, "Darling, you need to forgive them," but what they might really mean is, "It's time for you to act differently, because this is un-spiritual and it's bringing us down." Just look them in the eyes with a soft gaze and say, "I'm not ready. Please forgive me."

The preachy types might dispense forgiveness to other people as a superiority trip. The ego loves to bestow forgiveness on lesser fools. This is when beneath "I forgive you" lurks a little voice saying, "Gotcha! You were a loser and I forgive you, which makes me a winner." That's just a righteousness card trick—insecurity disguised as arrogance, disguised as spirituality.

The heart runs on its own clock, untethered from calendar days or years. A photographer friend was in major conflict with his daughter for about seven years. They rarely spoke. He showed up at our photoshoot with his gear and carrying the light stands behind him...was his daughter. Everybody on set who knew them was surprised; the crew just looked at each other like, *Ohhhkay. Act normal.* On a break, I said to her, "Um, so... you and your dad... THAT hatchet got buried, eh? What happened?" She smiled and nodded. "You know, we just decided to drop it. Just because. I said to him, 'You wanna drop it?' And he said, 'Ya, let's just drop it!' and we decided to..."—and then I said it with her—"Just drop it!"

Forgiveness can be a swift recovery, or not arrive until a generation later.

You will forgive when you are ready to forgive.

You can ply your Spirit with beautiful theologies. You can take solace from firsthand accounts of incredible, everyday people who forgave exceptionally horrible things. You can pray for the strength to turn the other cheek. And, I do hope for your sake and everyone else's that it's sooner rather than later, but...

You will forgive when you are ready to forgive.

How to begin the process of forgiveness

The *first* step: Forgive yourself for not wanting to forgive.

Who wants to forgive? Anger is so...so...right! Being right can feel so empowering! Empowerment feels like justice. Justice returns things to balance. Balance feels comforting. Comfort is so *mmmmm*—especially after pain.

Start there if you have to. *I don't want to forgive that S.O.B.* And because you're a Light worker, you will feel the weight of that resistance. You will naturally want relief—for both of you. So try this:

I forgive myself for not wanting to forgive.

The second step: Have the desire to forgive.

That's it. You don't need a plan. You don't have to estimate when you'll be ready to have lunch with them again, or if they're invited to your wedding. You don't have to think about what you'll say when you run into each other, or if you'll ever even speak again.

Just *want* to forgive and you'll be moving in the right direction.

Forgiving yourself

Self-forgiveness is a phenomenal freedom and all Love flows from there. I think self-forgiveness is our ultimate responsibility to others. Because when you forgive yourself, everyone implicated in the painful situation is liberated in some way.

We often worsen the bruises we receive from the outside world by delivering a second blow ourselves—self-judgment for putting ourselves in harm's way. *I shouldn't have been there. I should have been smarter, stronger, wiser, faster. Should have known better, been less sensitive, been more sensitive.*

And sometimes those should-haves are true. Even so, we have to forgive ourselves. *I forgive myself for being there. I forgive myself for not being smarter or stronger or wiser or faster.* Forgive yourself for quitting, for asking someone to do something that you knew was impossible for them to do, for taking more than your share. You're learning. You learned.

Forgiving others and forgiving ourselves is particularly tricky when the issue is one of betrayal—and so much human pain is the result of some form of betrayal.

Betrayal is such a defining experience—it lays your heart bare. In one fell swoop, betrayal highlights your beautiful loyalty and the lies you've been telling yourself. Being betrayed by another person is often (but not always) a reflection of how you were betraying yourself. It's a lie looking back at you.

It might be this simple: you were a fool because you were scared. You played dumb to get what you thought you needed. You kept one eye closed so you wouldn't have to face the pain of the situation.

So maybe you got blindsided. Now you see that perhaps you had a part to play in the betrayal (which in no way whatsoever lets the betrayer off the hook for being, say, connivingly parasitic, deceptive over a very long time, or a manipulative ass-face). And then, beneath the surface...you see that you were afraid of something.

Afraid of what? The answer to that is always personal. And that's where you change your story of betrayal into a story of forgiveness.

You're not discounting of the Truth of what happened or the realness of the pain. You're not erasing all the justifiable anger you felt in response to what happened—to do so would be to invalidate your heart's intelligence.

As Lady Ninja of the Light put it to me, "I see forgiveness as releasing congested energy that's not needed by the energy body. No stories, no players, simply time to release and move on to brighter ways."

You stop letting past hurt affect you in the present. You rinse down the story, you take what you want, and let the rest go up to the Light so it can be put to better use. *You give yourself forward.*

"All is forgiven" includes you.

When you're ready.

Nothing changes without you

10
THE SOUL OF SERVICE
Conscious optimism and giving from your fullness

Nothing changes without me

Sometimes, my heart is so open
I can't tell if it is a gaping wound
or a portal for everything that ever was and ever will be.

I've learned to Love the beautiful terror of eternity,
and scenario planning for how shattered I could be
if the dark things got tall
and if I fell backwards in my forgetting of the Light.

But you can't fall backwards in Space,
You can only only only ever unfurl.

More than anything,
I've wed the certainty that nothing changes without me—
not coal becoming diamonds
not fertilizing eggs
or migration patterns
or medicine dreams.

And what I thought was a net cast to me from a higher God
is actually strands of Truth and filaments of desire
that I have tied together with my own two hands.
And in precious encounters, I tie what I know and want to you,
so we can ride the winds of wonder.

Yes, and…

I arise in the morning torn between a desire to improve the world
and a desire to enjoy the world. This makes it hard to plan the day.
– E.B. White

I WRITE FROM A small room on the second floor of my house. On one recent morning, I took a moment to intentionally appreciate the amazing view: the green canopy of my neighbourhood with a fantastic downtown in the distance. Yo-Yo Ma playing Bach's Cello Suite No. 1 in G Major rolled through my stellar sound system. (Next to world peace, great speakers are all I've ever really wanted.) The sun was on my face. I get to write for a living.

And I thought, "All is well in the world."

Then I felt a contrasting darkness nudge me, about to rob me of that sweetly full moment. *But my kid is at his dad's place and I wish he were home this weekend. There's a serious heroin problem on the Downtown Eastside. That story I read last night about child brides in Senegal. Vaccines and autism. The shootings in Orlando…Nice…Istanbul…*

And I sighed, and thought, Yes, *and…*

Yes…and I'm going to be grateful. Yes…and I'm going to do all that I can to help. Light…and dark. Dark and…so much Light. Yes to the blessings. Yes to all that it means to be in this together.

Conscious optimism

I am driven by two main philosophies: know more today
about the world than I knew yesterday, and lessen the suffering
of others. You'd be surprised how far that gets you.
– Neil deGrasse Tyson

There are many reasons to feel hopeless about humanity's future, most of which come at you every morning as soon as you get online. A heaving ecosystem. Human trafficking. Gross divides in economic, racial, and gender equality—across the globe.

But according to a lot of spiritual perspectives, *all is well in the Universe. Our enlightenment is inevitable. It's all progress.*

I do believe that we will get to where we're headed—to a more enlightened way of living and co-creating. I fully buy into the notion that *all* is *well in the Universe. Our enlightenment* is *inevitable. It's all progress.*

I also believe that over-spiritualizing our global tragedies doesn't heal them—it perpetuates them. And I believe in free will. So we have a choice: stubborn ignorance can slow us down and make us take the long way 'round to our destination, or we can make some radical shifts and get there with some efficiency. The Universe operates on free will—and that means that both ascension and devolution are options. It's up to us.

I didn't watch the news for years. It was like, too negative. *What a downer.* I was really into this very popular New Age teacher who said that we should *only feed our minds positive information,* and therefore had sworn off all forms of news media. But that's not enlightenment. That's denial. And as a member of the collective, it's incredibly irresponsible. We need to know what's going on with each other.

And yes, the mainstream media are rabid fearmongers. The system is a conglomerated racket for creating profits through ratings and ad revenue. It's corporate-enforced, listener-supported brain-washing. The mainstream media "**manufactures consent**," as Noam Chomsky coined the practice—for wars, for policies, for rules of success. It paints a picture of us about our beliefs and behaviours that's one-dimensional and often wholly untrue. It hides the Light, the true positivity and sanity that's at work in the world. One result of news sensationalism is that it makes conscious citizens feel like outsiders and weighs on the hopeful. If more

Truth were broadcast, we might see that the majority of people have the intelligence and Love required to steward a healthy world.

Information is one form of power we can't tune out. We just need to listen more closely to hear what's real, while keeping our eyes on the enemies of Truth.

I'm an idealist, which by necessity means that I'm pissed off most of the time. I'm okay with being perpetually vexed because I think it's a sane—and potentially very productive—response to the times. Anger is better than apathy. Anger moves energy; apathy lets it calcify.

For many years, I focused on what I could do for the world from the astral plane—until I expanded my definition of "waking up" to include what I can do in the physical world.

We all need to wake up
so we can do the work
that needs to be done
to live in a world
that we espouse to want to live in.

Service is when spirit meets matter where it is. Service is being informed. Service is being enraged and compassionate. Service is being ruthlessly honest about the facts—*then* choosing to be hopeful about the future.

In the giving

It's not the load that breaks you down, it's the way you carry it.
– Lena Horne

By walking a spiritual path, we're signing up to be of service. And while the Love is usually genuine, it's useful to analyze our impulses to give, because self-helpers are primed to over-help.

When we give from emptiness or neediness, we're never as effectively helpful as we want to be. Over-the-top do-gooder work can be a coverup for low self-worth, and that can turn into unconscious martyrdom. Martyrdom can get twisted because beneath the do-gooding, one might be trying to get validation for their significance. We all deserve that kind of validation, but there are healthier ways to go about getting it.

Of course there are times when we give all we've got to give and collapse, euphorically spent and used up in our service. That all-out giving can be a beautiful thing. But if our insecurities drive us to give ceaselessly from an empty tank, there are some nasty consequences. First, if we wear ourselves out serving a cause, we just end up being a burden to someone else. We get sick, we get cranky, we're hard to rely on. Second, we might get so over-taxed that we stop genuinely caring about the cause we committed to. We're so numbed out that we don't see people anymore—we only see projects. We don't feel sympathy—we feel apathy. When we don't address our burnout, we become indifferent to ourselves and we lose our connection to the people we set out to serve in the first place.

Compassion, from Latin, means "to suffer with," and if healthy esteem and limits aren't in place, spiritual servants can get lost in that suffering. You see more patients than you should because someone's always in crisis, you work overtime to keep everyone's morale up, or you teach extra classes because your students praise your life-changing lessons. But your short-term giving turns into your long-term living. When you stop—by conscious choice or because your body or mind shuts down from exhaustion—you might realize that your own support system is pretty feeble. You haven't had time to explore your own interests (what were those extracurricular interests, anyway?), you have no idea where to go on holiday, and you might not have anybody you want to go with. Your cortisol levels are through the roof and your adrenals are baked.

You can only help when you can help. And maybe you can't help right now. Believing in an abundant Universe doesn't mean that you as an individual have an endless supply of energy to give away.

I think it was Mother Teresa who instructed us to "give until it hurts." I'd like to elaborate on that: Give until it hurts *so good*—not until it hurts you.

What is your giving taking from you?

I don't want you to stop giving. The world needs you to give. Generously. We need you to rise to meet the suffering of your surroundings. And to do that, we need you to be strong, healthy, and clear-minded. We need you to show up for the right reasons.

And we need you to trust in your community. Because when you need a break, someone will cover for you, and maybe learn what they're made of while trying to do so. Poet Tara Bracco reminisces on this kind of giving teamwork: "Remember in seventh-grade chorus class, when we all hummed one note? I envision an activism that's a sustained hum. When one person drops out, you don't notice, because everyone else continues." In between your giving, rest.

Where to start when you're feeling helpless

> *Today the planet is the only proper "in group."*
> *Participate joyfully in the sorrows of the world.*
> – Joseph Campbell

You have a golden heart, and this is your refrain:

I want to help. But how?

You hear tragic news about brutality and violence. You're moved to tears; you give it a moment or a few hours to sink in. Then, as you take a deep breath and switch your attention to the work of your day, you feel grey despair casting a shadow. It's as if hopelessness hovers over your heart, waiting for a cue to swoop right in and consume you. You still believe in the power of Love—you know that humanity has every kind of financial and intellectual resource to bring to bear on the situation. But in that moment, walking through the aftermath of yet another human tragedy, your strength stammers: *I want to help. But how?*

The fact of the global matter is that we are living, breathing, eating, and working in the aftermath of tragedy every day. We must constantly navigate through the mess that our collective greed and intolerance have created: post-traumatic stress syndrome, secondary stress syndrome, depression, hopelessness, violence. In her poignant book, *Tears to Triumph*, Marianne Williamson puts it this way: "Modern civilization has itself become a depressing phenomenon, predicated on principles that dissociate human beings from the feelings of connectedness and wholeness without which happiness cannot be found."

The pain—a psychic pain that most true hearts can attest to—is accumulating.

Where do you start when the world is so messed up and you're feeling messed up because of it?

Gloria Steinem offers some great advice: **work on what hurts the most**. Pick your issue. Pick any issue. Start by looking at the hard stuff. Feel the pain. Entertain despair. And then...pick a cause and apply your Love to it.

> How you live is how you lead, you know this. Your Love is your dominion—and it's enormous. YOU and that life of yours *are* the revolution.

Use your voice. Make some noise. Social media makes everyone a broadcaster. Use your platform, even if that platform is Thanksgiving dinner with your relatives. Annoy the shit out of people with how concerned you are. Be willing to be disliked. Don't let the pushback push you over. Dare to be idealistic. Something you say will stir a new thought that will lead to better action. The future is listening. Speak up.

Use your money. Tithing is a beautiful practice that's fallen out of fashion because so many of us don't attend places of worship where we might donate. Find a cause, consider it your church, and carve out a percentage of your paycheque for giving. (Even if you're just making ends meet, you probably won't miss two percent of your monthly take-home.) Come on. Do it. Step up. It's the consistency that's powerful—you're keeping your Love and attention flowing.

And hey, all you wellness entrepreneurs and empowerment bloggers: how about giving some dough in addition to airtime? When we create businesses with missions to make the world a better place, it's easy to think that we're already giving enough. Nope. Find a way to turn every product or project into both an awareness- AND money-raiser.

Use your body. Grab a hammer. Lift a box. Stuff envelopes. Sweat your prayers. In your next yoga class, instead of recapitulating your own pain from the day, devote every asana to grieving parents. Dance in your kitchen for the first responders, a dance of thanks. Dance out despair for the people who live in cultures where ecstatic movement is forbidden.

Use your Soul. Stop, drop, and send Light. You believe in it, so use it. After you dry your tears from the latest shooting or news headline, take four minutes—twenty if you can—to sit in silence and very specifically send Love, positive energy, healing, Light, and prayers to the person, people, place, or situation in need. How many times do we say to someone, "I'm sending Love"? Really send it.

Fill the in-between moments of your day by pouring your consciousness where it's needed.

Meditate on the move. Dedicate your subway ride to easing the pain of people with mental illness. Say this Buddhist invocation over and over again:

May all beings everywhere be happy and free. May the thoughts, words, and actions of my life today contribute to freedom and happiness for all.

Before you sleep, choose one person in your life and wish everything good for them. Burn a candle during breakfast for cancer fighters. Go for a walk, and instead of thinking about how to grow your business, give ten blocks and do a stream of consciousness to the planet: *may the oceans be purified, may the trees be revered, may the policymakers protect the atmosphere. Bless the soil, bless the sharks, bless the sidewalks, bless the garbage collectors, bless the bees. Heal us from pesticides, heal us from toxins, heal the nuclear meltdown sites. Love to the over-consumers, Love to the seed-keepers...*

Or create this simple meditation-invocation: speak aloud or think words that you direct at someone, some place, or the entire planet. *Peace. Understanding. Equality. Green. More beauty. Healthcare. Agreements. Fresh air. Loving parents. Connection. Recognition. Music. Kindness...*

Give the world your blessings as a mere mortal, just like any sainted, worshipped, appointed deity.

Before you leave a place, drop Light into the space with something like this: "May all who enter here be blessed with their heart's desire." Grocery stores, gas stations, public restrooms, classrooms, your neighbour's front porch—all space is opportunity for a blessing.

Bless all the babies born today. "May everyone see you and Love what they see." When you walk down the street, silently tell each person, "You can do it."

Be a conductor of deep acceptance. Outpour grace. When the situation overwhelms, let your Love take over.

Look for it

Look for Light with more intensity than ever. In all the density and confusion that's swirling on the planet, this is what it means to have Faith—Faith that you'll keep finding Light.

Don't waver in your gratitude for what is good and miraculous. Refuse to go numb. Instead, use questions to build your strength. You will get angry. Some days you will be devastated. But even on the days when you might fail to be compassionate, please don't let go of what you know in your bones: that compassion illuminates the darkness.

If you look with your Soul, you will keep finding Light everywhere.

you're the answer to your question

11

YOU ARE THE GURU
The hottest truth of all

We cannot live in a world that is not our own, in a world that is interpreted for us by others. An interpreted world is not a home. Part of the terror is to take back our own listening, to use our own voice, to see our own light.
– Hildegard of Bingen

Discipleshit

MY BUDDY ANGUS was house-sitting for a good friend of his, a very successful American businessman. Silicon Valley–type. Big house, hot tub overlooking a valley, and *white carpeting*. I was living in a 280-square-foot apartment at the time and it was the first time I'd ever been in a house with wall to wall *white carpeting*.

When I visited, I noticed that every single room of the gigantic home had an altar to the businessman's guru. In the office was an elaborate setup with guru photos, meditation cushions, and mala beads. Over the stove hung a laminated photo of the guru. I had a tinkle in the powder room and guess who was watching me? The guru, tacked above the towel rod, smiling.

Angus and I finished the house tour and sat down in front of the living room mantle, which had a very large gilded framed poster of—yep, you guessed it—the guru. I should mention that the closest I'd come to real altars before, other than the tabernacle in my Catholic church, was a high school pal's bedroom shrine to Duran Duran. These altars to the guru were altogether new and trippy, since the businessman was a very white, very three-piece-suit kind of guy who drove a Volvo. And the guru was a very East Indian man with a sizeable afro who was to always smiling and wearing a bright orange full-length tunic. One of these things was not like the other.

We sunk into the reclining chairs in front of altar number thirty-nine. Angus looked at the guru setup, looked at me, and in his cockney accent, said, "So whaddya you make a' that then?" We'd just smoked a big joint, so my inner editor was definitely off-duty. I rolled my eyes and said, referring to the man whose home we were gently invading, "What a total tool!" Giggles ensued and Angus said, "It's a bit much, innit?" And he leaned in to whisper, I guessed partly out of respect for his friend and partly in case the avatar was eavesdropping, "You know, he doesn't make a decision without asking the guru first—like where to go on 'oliday, even." And we laughed our stoned faces off and slunk back to the kitchen to hunt for ice cream.

A few years later, another good friend rang me up and said, "Hey, have you ever heard of Sathya Sai Baba?" I sure had. "The swami with the 'fro and the orange dress. Ya, I know him."

"Well, pack your bags. We're going to India." I had to see for myself. Within a month I was walking through his ashram gates, with frangipani flowers in my hair.

Kneeling

Much like the toddler musical prodigy who shocks her parents when she bangs out a concerto on her toy piano, some "gurus" start to exhibit a genius-level knowledge of esoteric principles in childhood. As they grow into their calling, supernatural powers sometimes emerge, like capacities for bilocation and healing, dream visitation, incredible psychic awareness, and material manifestation. Then come reports from their community of the euphoria and healing that people experience in their presence.

As someone raised in western world Catholicism, Jesus Christ was my central reference point for spiritual superheroism. When it became clear that he was not the only human with the capacity to walk on water and multiply loaves and fishes, I was thrilled. Not because my Christ adoration was in question, but because I loved the idea of democratic, divine power distribution—a world blessed with many miracle workers, unknown and emerging, witnessed and well-documented.

Now, if you start investigating swamis, you'll quickly figure out that controversy loves them. Magical capacities, throngs of devotees, sizeable donations, elaborate temples—gurus can be lightning rods for salacious stories. Sai Baba was a classic example. He was known for his miracles. I have skeptical friends who witnessed his magic for themselves. Baba would twirl his hand a few times, *et Voila!* Out of his palm would drop a gold chain, which he then placed over the head of a very awed temple visitor—many of them, in succession. Major bling time. (You can watch it on YouTube and judge for yourself.)

In addition to being praised for his powers, his messages of Love and selfless service, and his first-rate university and hospital (people journey from as far as New Jersey to India for open-heart surgery at no cost), Sai Baba was accused of being a con man and sexual predator with a special preference for young men. This didn't stop the flow of visitors to his various temples.

On my first day at his ashram, I arose at four a.m. to stand in line at the grand temple entrance. It was sublime. Roosters crowed over the mantras wafting from tinny speakers, and a peachy glow blanketed the dusty laneways. The collective anticipation of meeting Baba was shimmery and sweet. I paid a few rupees to choose some flowers from a basket of blossoms. And, I'm embarrassed to say, I even wore a bindi on my forehead.

(Which is kind of like being a white girl on holiday in Jamaica and getting cornrows. Lame.)

No eye contact between opposite genders is allowed within the ashram walls. If you're caught glancing, you can be sure that one of the elderly women will snap her fingers in your face to avert your gaze. Hundreds and hundreds of men and women file in separately to the temple.

That week, I fell into the order of things. I chanted. I prayed. I meditated. I watched, carefully. And while I can now say that being a devotional novice probably skewed my perspective, my thought at the time was, *This is joyless.* I tried to find it, but I could not get a hold on much bliss while I was there. The group of Germans visiting in their new white tunics seemed pompous to me. There was never laughter in the air. During mornings at the temple as Sai Baba shuffled by us in our neat, kneeling rows, some devotees with gaping mouths and apparently euphoric faces just made me cringe inside. I was eager and open-minded; I wanted a transmission to elevate my Soul. But all I kept thinking was, *You poor things.*

On my final day, the woman kneeling next to me was one such ecstatic follower. She was from the East Coast of the U.S. "When did you arrive?" I asked her, in a whispered voice. "Three years ago." she said. "You mean your first visit was three years ago, or you've been here for three years?" I asked, my head tilted a bit. "Oh, I got here and never left," she said, glowing. She had received a letter from Sai Baba—who does not sit down and write random letters in English to women on the eastern seaboard, so this was evidently a divinely materialized letter—that arrived smelling of frangipani flowers. The letter told her to come to India to be in his presence. "So I left my husband and children and came to be with father Baba," she sighed, dreamily. Okay, now this was getting interesting.

"Wow. How old are your kids?" I asked. She was so tripped out that she didn't seem to realize that I was judging her good and hard, the single, childless tart that I was at the time. "They're twelve and fifteen." I thought I'd give her mothering skills the benefit of the doubt and asked, "Have they been here?" She shook her head no. "Nuh-uh. Nope," she said. I just didn't know what to say to that, so I smiled softly and bowed my head in prayer formation with the crowd.

I wasn't at the ashram long but, as it happens for me in any situation of extreme restraint, I started feeling hornier than usual, and craving other circumstantially illicit things like a pack of smokes and some Led Zeppelin cranked really loud. Oh woe. My mind was having a fairly predictable reaction to discipline, but so was my heart. It was becoming clear that I was not made for this scene.

A taste of rapture

Sai Baba would be one of many gurus and sages that I would visit over the years. While I did not feel a connection with him or his environment, I did have, and continue to have, incredibly positive and effectual experiences with other spiritual teachers and masters. It was perfect that my explorations into the dynamics of discipleship would begin with experiences of suspicion and disconnection—it kept me alert in a critical way.

Still, I hungered for miracles and to be overcome with transcendental awareness downloaded to me from a luminous human being. I was to get a taste of the rapture I was craving.

One such experience happened at a gathering in Santa Fe, New Mexico, with Karunamayi, a swamini affectionately called "Amma" (not to be mistaken with the popular "Hugging Saint" who also goes by Amma). She had been interpreting Sanskrit spiritual verses since she was a small girl. That summer night in a community centre, she spoke of a Love that carries all, the God Head Love that bears everything for its creation. My friend Navjit and I planned to take in her darshan, then head out clubbing afterward. So there we sat, lotus style, in our pleather pants and Timberlands, as eager for the satsang as we were for dancing all night long.

"My children, my babies," Amma said in her soft pitch and heavy Indian accent. "When you are angered, give your anger to Mama. Mama will carry it for you. When you do not know, give your confusion to Mama. Mama will carry it for you." Give my unresolved and destructive content over to God? Aren't we supposed to repair and polish, and then present our positivity and diligence to the Creator? Just give my anger upward? As an overachieving, recovered Catholic, this was hard for me to grok.

When it came time for the laying on of hands, I shyly queued up for Amma's blessing. Everyone ahead of me was quiet and composed. I wasn't expecting much to happen. But when she put her hands on my bowed head I immediately began to cry, tears trailing cobalt-blue mascara down my cheeks. It was as if her touch on the crown of my head had turned on a tap. The best word to describe the indescribable feeling was *cradled*. The only thought I could articulate was, *This is what it is to be carried by God.*

In the blessing of a lifetime, I was once given the opportunity, along with five other friends, to meet with the Dalai Lama. After a free-flowing Q&A full of bursts of laughter and philosophy, His Holiness hugged each one of us goodbye and in doing so, took a moment to gaze directly into our eyes. I have never experienced anything like it. I swear I saw outer space in his eyes, and not just a "twinkle in his eye" quality, but vastness itself. That gaze was a transmission of lovingkindness that I'm sure stemmed from eternity. The exchange gave me a sense of the timelessness of real Love—a quality that then became aspirational for me. With one look, His Holiness had completely recalibrated my standards for relating to humanity. The standards of which seem impossibly high for an everyday human with hang-ups—but the only thing worth aiming for.

From *cradled* to *vastness*. The Holy Feminine to the Holy Masculine. From stories of slander and scandal to witnessed miracles. My eager heart pressed on with the search for true masters...cautiously.

The science of surrender

The Lord Buddha has said that we must not believe in a thing
said merely because it is said; nor traditions because they
have been handed down from antiquity; ...nor writings by
sages, ...nor on the mere authority of our teachers or masters.
But we are to believe when the writing, doctrine, or saying
is corroborated by our own reason and consciousness.

– H.P. Blavatsky, *The Secret Doctrine:*
The Synthesis of Science, Religion, and Philosophy

Who better to ask about guru worship than a guru himself? Guru
Singh is a third-generation American yogi, and for twenty years was the
protégé of Yogi Bhajan, the guru who introduced Kundalini yoga to much
of the western world. In my estimation, he's the real deal. I have such a
full-hearted respect for what he teaches, how he teaches it, and mostly,
how he treats people.

"Guru" is a Sanskrit word. Guru Singh beaks down the definition: "'Gu'
means darkness—darkness in which there's no light—as in ignorance and
confusion. 'Ru' means light in which there's no darkness—the opposite
of darkness, light and clarity. Therefore, the word 'guru' means to light
the darkness, someone who teaches how darkness can be illumined, one
who sheds light on your ignorance."

As is customary for Sikhs of his stature, Guru Singh is always dressed in
tunic and a turban. The day we meet, he wears all white with a turquoise
scarf. As is customary for me, I'm in skinny jeans, with big hair.

"Can you talk about the dynamic of devotion?" I ask him. "Does devo-
tion require one to give themselves over to another's authority? Because..."
I steeled my gaze as if to say, *c'mon, that can't be right.* He got my drift.
Guru Singh always gets the drift.

"Devotion is the science of surrender. It's a state without blocks or
barriers. An 'object-free' quality, not directed toward anyone, or anything.

And when you're without barriers, you absorb all the knowledge that's available in the moment."

In other words, it's not about the guru themselves. It's much, much, bigger. This is a paradigm-busting concept for many worshippers who may have hung their hopes for illumination on a singular master.

I nod my head, engrossed. Guru Singh delivers information in an almost musical cadence; you never feel flooded or strung along. It's like a song with a beginning, middle, and end. "When you're in a state of devotion, you have zero defenses, and therefore you absorb absolutely everything. Devotion in the presence of a 'guru' absorbs the 'guru's' talents."

Consider the profound subtlety of this. Gurus and spiritual authorities are often positioned and perceived as the dispensers of wisdom. This can create a setup where the devotee must be deemed worthy of the dispensation. The gifts may or may not be bestowed—it all depends on the guru's opinion.

Yet again, this positions us on the outside, trying to earn our way in, which is a very different energy than opening ourselves up to more knowledge. The former is externally motivated; the latter is internally inspired.

Working for approval takes up a lot of energy, and it can be a huge distraction from seeing the gifts that you already hold in your hands.

Let's imagine this interaction literally. You're sitting before a truly great, spiritually gifted being—a guru. You face each other in silence, your eyes closed.

First, imagine yourself trying to earn a blessing from them. Here's what you might project outward, with all of your might and energetic sway: *See me, see me. I'm giving you Love. Can you feel my goodness? Please bless me. Do you feel me?* Cloying anxiety arises in you, pulling your attention to your hunger for approval. You focus on how much you want to be given something; you keep seeing your lack. This creates fatigue, messes with your ability to concentrate, and blocks your ability to receive that which you want most.

Now, let's shift the intention of your attention. You're sitting across from a great being... And you're not trying to get anything from them. No approval, no information. You're simply...open. In fact, you are intensely devoted to being open. This is the state of surrender. And from this spacious, faithful awareness, you can receive whatever wants to be given to you. What's more important, you can feel what already exists within you. You have just unfurled into Possibility with a capital P.

This enables an *exchange* of power. As Guru Singh puts it, the guru "is the map...you're the witness. They ignite the master inside of you." No one can give you fire to carry. But when the conditions are right, they can stoke the fire that's already within you—the Light, the G*uru*.

Ultimately, we are surrendering to the opportunity to become our masterful selves.

Power struggles

Devotion and power, leader and follower...so much can go wrong. There are spiritual superhumans, there are magicians, and there are luminous leaders. Some people work for the Light, others...others do their work in the shadows.

I actually believe that skilled esoteric technicians can pull objects out of thin air—gold chains and otherwise. Not with a slight-of-hand, David Copperfield trick, but through the true manipulation of dimensions, bringing the abstract into dense formation. I wholeheartedly believe that there are gifted humans who can walk through walls, bilocate, perform psychic surgeries, and cure the supposedly incurable. Multidimensional manipulation. Inexplicable miracles.

But…just because someone can create so-called "miracles" doesn't mean that they have pure intentions. Metaphysical skill does not guarantee spiritual integrity.

Some well-branded apparent Light workers are just darkness peddlers in disguise. They know how to plug into other people's energy to get a boost for themselves or to create an effect—maybe a healing effect. Of these types of people Nietzsche might have said, "They muddy the waters to make it seem deep." Where the healer types are involved, you might get "healed" in one area of your body or life, but then something goes wrong elsewhere. It's like super-charging a car battery but draining the oil at the same time—you get an injection of energy but something is *not quite right with the overall system.*

So, don't let mad meta-skillz impress you. Great healing and insight capacities are exquisite gifts, but we have to peer behind the curtain to determine the wizard's purity of intention. Quality is so hard to identify in this space. You have to learn to see with both your heart and your intellect, cultivating Faith while questioning ceaselessly. It's more important for you to believe in your powers of discernment than someone else's healing powers.

For example, let's look at some of the spiritual heroes of the last century. Mahatma Gandhi was an icon of peace and non-violent communication, right? Well, Gandhi also had some rather unorthodox sexual behaviours. Allegedly, to test the vow of chastity he took when he was thirty-eight, though he was married, he called on young women, including his niece, to sleep naked with him. He also set up ashrams where he ran experiments of purity—boys and girls were to bathe and sleep together, chastely, but were punished for any sexual talk. Well, that's one way to practice being a pacifist.

There's much evidence that the Reverend Dr. Martin Luther King, Jr. had a number of extramarital affairs. "We all understood and believed in the Biblical prohibition against sex outside of marriage," wrote his closest comrade, Ralph David Abernathy. "It was just that he had a particularly difficult time with that temptation." As for Mother Teresa, some academics scrutinized the medical care that her patients received—which was inexcusably shoddy—and concluded that she had a tendency of "caring for the sick by glorifying their suffering instead of relieving it."

Every hero wants to stay a hero.

On one hand, having flaws doesn't make you a fraud; it makes you human. No one's perfect, so we shouldn't expect our heroes to be. We put gurus and spiritual leaders on pedestals because we want hope—hope of being rescued from the mess we're in. We might look to our radiant yoga instructor as a model to lead us out of our lethargic and angsty reality, or we might hang on the words of a motivational speaker for the how-to on fearless living. And if the people we're adulating are truly on the same level that we are, that they are simultaneously awesome *and* flawed—then it means we're all in this muddle together. This isn't quite as comforting as the idea of someone leading us out of the darkness to the Promised Land.

> Some religious leaders get a little carried away with luxury living. Some cultural revolutionaries break their vows of fidelity. The yogini has dark and disembodied days. Does that mean that the perfectly spiritual, humanitarian role model does not exist? Yep. That's exactly what it means.

On the other hand, how can we have grace for the humanity of spiritual leaders while holding them to impeccable standards at the same time? We have to sense our togetherness at the deepest level. We need to make dignity and grace an intention. It's staggering how base even sane citizens can behave in the fight for morality...casting our stones and getting all opinionated from behind our computer screens. We need to make our definitions of "leader and follower," "sage and seeker" more malleable—we are all both. It's essential to have visionaries in the lead, but we need to expect more from ourselves and in some respects, less from those at the helm. So that when (not *if*) our regarded leaders make a misstep, we have the wherewithal to hold them accountable, then uphold the vision we shared—or to create a new one in its place.

What happens when a spiritual leader violates the sacred relationship they have with their followers? Well, according to Guru Singh and most well-measured esoteric advisors, "There's a huge karmic debt waiting for the teacher." Also known by Christians as *a special place in hell.* If you've been on the receiving end of the abuse of power, this may or may not be of some consolation. I've been on the other side of breached metaphysical trust. When my rage eventually receded, I felt immense compassion for the astral felon, because they had sentenced themselves to some serious spiritual cleanup duty—they had a towering list of amends to make. And then some.

Holding leaders accountable for destructive behaviour can tear communities and families apart. Accountability can bring down a nation. But, whistleblowers, Truth crusaders, and activists need to see themselves as the healers that they are. And healing usually involves disruption. What happens if the whole commune or council falls apart because corruption is brought to Light? People snap out of their illusions and learn to stand on their own—at least that's the invitation.

Raising your voice can be as treacherous as it is liberating. Devotion to the Truth will demand everything of you. When you stand for your Soul, you become the leader we all need.

Romanticizing the exotic

I stood at the back of a Buddhist temple in the northern hills of India, soaking in the monks' melodic chants. It was late afternoon; the sun was heavy gold. The young monks at the front were ten or twelve years old; they rocked back and forth, eyes fixed on the meditation scrolls. It was mesmerizing and, at the same time, disturbing. I wondered if they all truly wanted to be there. At that age, did they accept it as positive or negative karma that their mothers gave them over to the monastery to live out their lives as monks? I wondered who of the lot would grow up and want to bust out.

Many years later, I visited an Ayurvedic doctor in California, a revered practitioner from India. He had the warm smile, round glasses, and features of a very brown, wrinkled John Denver. And great style. A white t-shirt, 501s, Blundstone boots, and an old ruby ring that swiveled around his finger.

We sat in his living room talking about the characteristics of my dosha type (Pitta Kapha, obviously), and I took the first opportunity I saw to ask him a few questions about his life.

"I heard that you used to be a monk when you were in India." I put it right out there, hoping he wouldn't think I was too intrusive. "Yes, yes," he nodded. "Why did you leave?" I asked. "Before I began, I was working with the Prime Minister. But I saw that the promises being made were not being kept. This leads to bad karma. I could not go on any longer like this." He put his hand up to gesture *stop!* Needless to say, I was riveted. *You had me at "Prime Minister."*

"So I left and became a monk. But then I saw many things that were, you know, creepy within the monks and the boys." I interjected. "I always wondered about that. If it's happening with the Catholic priests, it's got to be happening with Tibetan monks." He grimaced. "Yes, yes. There is abuse."

He continued, "I was there because I was interested in the *alchemical*, in turning sulphur into gold. I wanted to bring my science to the mysticism. But this community had a lot of dirt in it. I walked through the dirt to get what I wanted." And he shrugged and looked at me like, *And THAT's how it's done.* I leaned forward to give him a fist bump, but he didn't recognize the gesture and it turned into an awkward high-five.

Same blessings, same curses, just different temples. Exotic lands and intriguing rituals aren't necessarily more effective than what's in your own backyard or the church you grew up in.

We've got to talk about False Prophets

We're living in an era that Sanskrit scriptures call Kali Yuga, "the age of vice." (Not to be mistaken with the righteous kick-ass Goddess Kali; this is altogether different.) Scholars can't agree on the actual timelines of various eras, but it's safe to say that each era lasts many centuries. We've moved through the Golden Age (happiness and Truth!) to the Silver Age (not as much happiness and Truth) to Bronze (um, way less happiness and Truth), and we are now in the Iron Age, the Kali Yuga (Hey! Where'd all the happiness and Truth go?!) Warning: if you're struggling to be optimistic about the state of humanity, you might want to skip this part altogether.

Because, I quote, "Kali Yuga is the age of darkness and ignorance. Society falls into disuse and people become liars and hypocrites. Knowledge is lost and scriptures are diminished. Humans eat forbidden and dirty food and engage in unrestrained sinful sexual practices. The environment is polluted, water and food become scarce. Wealth is heavily diminished. Brahmanas [the teachings of priests] become ignorant, Kshatriyas [the warrior caste] become weak, Vaishyas [merchants and farmers] employ questionable business tactics and Shudras [the worker caste] treacherously acquire power. Families become non-existent." And this is my favourite zinger, "Hypocrisy will be accepted as virtue."

Is this looking vaguely familiar?

The good news is that it's a great time to be a Light worker. I mean, you *knew* you were here for a reason, but let me tell you, you're an essential services worker, sweetheart.

Here's why I bring this up. As many spiritual leaders believe, with this darkness comes a proliferation of False Prophets. Energy suckers and money takers. Fakers. This has been picking up speed for centuries, but in very recent times, thanks to the internet and Photoshop, and some basic business skills, anybody can be well-branded and accumulate a lot of followers in their ashrams and on their Facebook pages. They are certified, sometimes very talented, and appear to know what they're talking about. They come in all denominations and domain names.

But what about the cosmic masters who are staggeringly dedicated to creating more Light on the planet, who have gleaned truly valuable knowledge that throngs of people would cherish, but who don't have a slick website or a publicist on retainer? These are folks who spend much of their time in reflection and repose, and wouldn't know the first thing about finding a virtual assistant. They may be trickling their content onto the internet, but it's next to impossible to hear them through the din of bestseller lists, search engine algorithms, podcast reviews, and other popularity contests.

How to tell a poser from a true teacher? Listen for the *real* story. True teachers freely share their backstory; you won't have to go digging for it. They will speak honestly and frequently of their personal, genuine pain—a pain that is both isolating and very much connected to their Love of humanity. And they will speak modestly and reverently of the gifts that came with their struggle and search. They are not simply reorganizing other people's ideas into a new, shiny package and shouting about it. They took their own path to inner knowing and found the Universal within. While they may stand upon other mystical ideas and teachings, their how-tos come from *living through it*. And they certainly aren't solely driven by clicks or cash. They aren't preaching; they are practicing.

Resonating with the Truth

> *If what I say resonates with you,*
> *it is merely because we are both branches of the same tree.*
> – W.B. Yeats

Here's what happens almost every time I do a speaking gig. I try to dispense some luminous Truthbombs and how-to advice—because that's what I've been invited there to do. I make fun of myself. I usually mention something about *reframing your obligations into conscious choices,* and *what you stop doing is just as important to your success as what you start doing.* I dish some inappropriate jokes, make note of my killer shoes, and then I probably mention that having some form of stillness or contemplative practice in your life is a really good idea.

And then it happens. Someone grabs the roving mic, theoretically to ask a question, but really, they're frustrated with me because I haven't made things any easier for them. They respectfully object, "But I have *real* obligations…" "But I am super busy…" "But I get really anxious when I sit down to meditate…so now what do you suggest?"

Here's what I used to do in those situations. I'd scramble. I'd try to keep up the energy in the room and I'd try to be extra encouraging. I'd attempt to rock out just one more wisdom nugget so I looked infinitely wise. I could feel myself spin out a bit, away from my centre. I noticed that answering one of those "but *now* what?" questions was one of the rare times that I'd lose my train of thought on stage. *What was I saying?*

What I *wanted* to say was this:

"For the Love. I can't solve all your problems from up here. In fact, I can't solve any of them. Go easy on me. And, newsflash: life is really really hard and I never said this consciousness business was easy. You gotta work for it, babe."

Because, honestly, I don't think that I can *truly* help anyone. Not really. No matter how much insight or sweat I give, the effects of my giving aren't within my control. I have nothing to do with someone receiving my Love or Light—it's the choice of the Loved. If someone runs with my idea, or is moved, or takes my suggestion and turns their life around, that's because of their readiness and wisdom, not mine. I can only show up with a sincere heart and hope that I reach you at just the right micro-moment with the perfect dose of Light that helps you see what you already know.

The motivational speaker gives you the "a-ha" you've been craving for years. Relief! The guru delivers the answer. *Om Shanti!* You read the answer you needed in a book and it cracks your mind open. Insight! Your shrink helps part the seas of your confusion. *What would I do without you?!*

Your breakthroughs have more to do with your own power than that of the expert or guru.

Outside sources can be Soul resources—but not because THEY know something that you don't. They are merely showing you your own wisdom. Wisdom is built, not bestowed.

It's all about resonance. Teachers (in all forms) hold up a mirror for you in just the right Light, and you catch your reflection in it.

Your Truth collides with theirs for a eureka moment.
This means you get to reframe your learning from:

"He gave me the answer."
To: "He said something that I knew was true."

"She's so wise."
To: "Her wisdom really resonated with me."

"They are the experts."
To: "This really fits with my own strengths."

This way, you fully respect your teachers. *Deep bow.* And you respect your innate wisdom. Ever unfolding. You had the ears to hear it. You showed up at the right time. You are *attuned.*

The thing about advice

One solution doesn't fit every problem (although many "wisdom empires" are built upon a single, general methodology). My observation of true wisdom is that it's often delivered with humility *and* boldness. Unflappable confidence *and* room for change. Most great teachers will hit these notes:

- Everyone is different, but we're all the same.
- One size does not fit all.
- What works for you today might not be what's best for you tomorrow.
- It made sense at the time.
- You grew into it, and you'll probably grow out of it.
- Nothing matters; everything is important.
- This works for me; it may or may not work for you.
- It depends.

So...keep looking until you find what works for you.

Don't deny it

Man, sometimes it takes you a long time to sound like yourself.
- Miles Davis

Right or wrong, pass or fail, winner or loser.

In charge. Not in charge.

Most social and religious systems reward conformity with approval and access. We're trained from the beginning of our lives, in almost every organized endeavour, to look outside of ourselves for the right answer. Our parents, teachers, and leaders ask it of us. And then we carry on the tradition and ask it of others: *Please meet my expectations.* It's a snarled up mass of illusions and dogma, laced with the sublimely universal human need to be comforted and to *have an effect*.

So if you're looking at your life and thinking, *Eeeshk, I've just been going along for the ride*, go easy on yourself. The status quo is a ubiquitous racket. And you can get off the merry-go-round at any time. Now would be good. It's always the right time to trust yourself.

Start with going on an "input fast." Give yourself three months, maybe six months of, say, no "readings" of any kind (unless they're poetry readings). No predictive astrology readings, ixnay on the psychics, nada on the tarot cards. If you're not in crisis mode right now, you might even consider taking a hiatus from your coach and/or your therapist. You could cut all external advice out of your daily diet. Might do wonders for your skin.

The silence of the advice-free zone may be deafening for a while, but do you hear that? It's you speaking. Directly to...you. It's your body telling you what it immediately knew and has known for a long time (because your body always knows). It's your very own perceptivity rising to the surface of your life. And it knows what it's talking about.

So maybe you're not channeling Spirit Guides verbatim every morning. And so what if you don't know what past-life karma is playing out in your business, or what the next lunar eclipse portends? You'll probably know enough to decide what's best for you on that given day. And you can keep flexing your own intuition (because it's just like a muscle) to feel into the next right step. Of course you're going to take wrong turns and get yourself into big shit-pickles. But an even bigger mistake would be to deny the power within you for the rest of your life.

the sacred
flourishes
with respect

12
FAUX FREEDOMS
When sacred sex goes sideways

I LOVE WEDDINGS. I Love the Love, the happy tears, and the drunken uncles. I even Love the bad DJs. I especially Love the lady power when we huddle up over the linen tablecloths and get down to getting real.

"How's it going with Jack?" one of us asks Sara. "Great, ya great," she says, glancing away at the twinkly lights draped from the rafters.

But you can't fool your girls. "How's it *really* going?" I ask. "Yeah, how's it *really* going?" one of the other girls echoes. At this point, the four of us are barefoot and we're good and sweaty after crushing "Blister in the Sun" on the dance floor. We look at Sara. We're waiting.

"Well, he wants to do the open relationship thing. And we've been going really fucking deep with the Tantra. You guys, it's SO hot. I feel really close to him." But then Sara's energy dips way down. "I think opening up the relationship could be our next edge. But, I dunno." She shrugs.

One of us is a life coach (of course). Life Coach says to Sara, "How does that make you feel?" One of us is a channeller/nutritionist (of course). Channeller says, "Do you feel called to have an open relationship?" One of us is me, and I say, "Well you don't seem too fucking turned on by the idea."

"Well, we met a *bunch* of poly couples at Burning Man," Sara reports.

Life Coach: "Who *isn't* poly at Burning Man?" We laugh so loud that the dudes standing at the open bar look over at us, fully suspecting that this joke's on them. We bat our eyelashes and carry on.

Sara: "And some of them have been together for a long time. With kids, even."

Channeller: "'Long time' is a relative term."

Me: "Well, all of my shrinks say that open never fucking works. You can make it work for a while, sometimes a long while even, but it's always the outside pull that unravels it."

Life Coach: "You really would be okay with him banging another woman?"

Sara: "I mean...well...I want to reeeally expand, you know. We gotta keep taking things to the next level. But...NO. I'd rather that he *not* get it on with anyone else. Like, ever. It's just..."

Me: "It's just OFF, is what it is. You are so not into this. If you seemed into it we'd be all like, *Yeah! Go for it!* Actually, I'm lying; I'd totally try to talk you out of it. But you do *not* seem into this."

Life Coach: "I bet you can find a way to relate even more deeply to each other within your comfort zone."

Channeller: "You gotta respect your Shakti, sister."

Me: "Fucking rights."

We've all suffered—women and men, hetero, homo, fluid, or undecided —under thousands of years of patriarchy that continues to propagandize that human bodies are commodities and property of the governing power.

If you control someone's sexuality, you seize control of their life. Between oppressive culturalization and the shifting expressions of feminism, I get why Yoni Puja empowerment workshops or an orgy at Burning Man might be appealing—truly healing, even. For some of us, getting greased and going wild is exactly what we need to break the psychological chains and move up our own evolutionary spiral.

I also understand why so many progressive, spiritually-focused women think they might look like prudes if they demur on the free love. It can be easy to feel ever-so-slightly shamed for not being "freer," as if they're repressed just because they don't want to go to the Proud and Powerful Pussy Power Summit and pair up with a guy they just met to find their orgasmic sweet spot.

What *is* the modern goddess to do?

Going wild isn't necessarily freeing.

And restraint isn't always restrictive.

> *Where does it begin*
> *When you love somebody?*
> *Maybe it's that moment when*
> *We leave our bodies*
> *And become*
> *Something more than what we see*
> - Active Child, "These Arms"

Freeing our bodies, messing with our minds

Groupthink is difficult to detect in the self-help space because it's often spun as progressive and undogmatic. It shimmers with a counter-culture glow. It's especially complicated when liberal content is aimed at our sexuality, where vulnerability and power intertwine so intricately. On top of all that, most of us live in cultures that tout hyper-sexualization as empowerment. *Look how uninhibited she is. She is* owning *it.* Very possibly, yes. Or maybe she's letting a broken system dictate her worth.

It's confusing. Just when you get your feminist profile in order, you might have to figure out where your spirituality fits into it.

If I'm meditating to transcend my desires, can I still want to be ravaged by my lover? Where does erotica meet purity? If I'm a feminist, do I have to like porn?

It's all so personal. So very, very personal.

> *How you like infinity disclosed is a matter of taste.*
> – David Deida

From my perspective, I see some ladies in goddess costumes and guys banging on djembe drums who may be masking some unresolved need for Love and attention. The herd mentality in sex liberation circles is as strong as any other, and in that environment, boundaries can be judged as sex-negative instead of sex-positive; discomfort can be labelled as rigidity.

It's healthy to rebel against oppression, but rebelliousness for its own sake can create another trap. And in that snare, where our natural cravings for Love and acceptance are enflamed, we make a lot of weird things "acceptable" so that we can gain acceptance. But trust me—your "no" can be as life-affirming as your "yes."

In all the cross-pollination (and commodification) of global ancient wisdom, "sacred sex" and Tantra teachings are likely the most mutilated. Tantra in the West is currently a fucking mess. Pun intended. Centuries-old Tantra training requires its students to undergo years of rigorous contemplative practice and "emptying of the self"—something that is scarcely mentioned in sacred sexuality workshops these days. In some lineages, sharing what you practice with your Tantric partner is strictly forbidden, but now, anyone can google how-to sexual positions and Tantra techniques. Broader access to hallowed wisdom isn't inherently bad; it's just that the techniques, when applied without any philosophical understanding, can be used as a distraction from true intimacy and illumination.

> When the "sacred" gets stripped out of "sacred sex," we're no longer safe to release the energy in our hearts. We lose the compassionate motivation that's the "Light" within "enlightened connection." That Light can express itself in lovemaking in a way that is so soft and simple that you float into Spirit, or in a hot, unbridled lust that grinds into grateful oneness.

All spiritual effort is movement toward Truth. There's more than one way to tap that transcendent state where you meet the bliss that pulses within reality. And (not surprisingly) when you bring up sexuality as a means of enlightenment, opinions polarize faster than you can say "Let's get it on."

We're all too familiar with the religious paradigms that blame sex for blocking enlightenment. Immaculacy is hammered into religious doctrine, and vows of chastity are part of many ordained religious positions. Even for laypeople following a strict meditative path, renunciation is usually part of the deal.

In contrast, some esoteric schools of thought believe that sex is the most direct route to spiritual liberation. Taoist yoga master Mantak Chia says, "You can either pray one hundred thousand hours, or you can consciously guide sexual energy up the spine." Which is to say, why sit solo in lotus position for years when you can find the cosmos in a properly handled orgasm?

Some Tantric texts say that the Buddha did not attain enlightenment during his years wandering and meditating under the banyan tree, as is widely told. Instead, he reached nirvana through his sexual relationship with his wife, well before he renounced his royal lifestyle and took to the woods. It's thought that he went forth as an already-enlightened being and that his public, contemplative lifestyle was, in part, a means to inspire people to embark on their own spiritual voyage.

You can find other such radical religious interpretations within Christian mysticism. Some esoterically inclined researchers believe that Mary Magdalene was not a common village prostitute, but that she was a high-level Tantric initiate, and that she and Jesus were engaged in a committed, profoundly sacred and sexual relationship. And what's more, their devotion and alchemy was a crucial power source for Christ's miraculous capacities. Mmm hmmm.

So even if we trace to the very roots of the pro-abstinence paradigm and the pro-sex liberationists, eventually it all gets dirty...sexy...sacred... pure, and back 'round to the puritanical.

Seeing sex as a primary means to spiritual attainment is problematic because it requires us to rely on someone else for our advancement. On the other end of the spectrum, life-long abstinence is fraught with the dangers that come from suppressing sensual desire.

I know that my idea of sexual empowerment has, at times, looked prudish to other people in my life. I once had an ordained monk tell me that I needed more vices. But since he really liked his weed and the ladies, I didn't take it to heart. And I'm sure that some of the most Soul-affirming things I've done looked total Super Whore to others.

Holding out, putting out...it's so very, very personal. My liberation comes from the restraints of my standards. My boundlessness and daring, my shocking vulnerability and oceanic strength can unfurl because of a sacred container I've put into place. I'm clear: I want to be fucked open to God. I want to find that dark place that is not the absence of Light, but rather, space itself. And I want to make Love and Light in that infinite space. Sacred communion. Communion as service. And that kind of sexy requires some deep fucking devotion—which, in my experience, is always worth holding out for. The sacred flourishes, wildly so, with respect and discernment. And discernment by its very nature creates limits. Those limits can pave the inroads to freedom.

Love meets you where you're at. No coercion. No judgments. A loving heart can temper the right amount of smut with spirit. Nowhere is this more evident in my life than in the sex advice that my girlfriends and I give each other. If you don't have some vagina-reverent women friends in your life, please go make some right away. This invitation extends to all fundamentally genitalia-adoring, sexuality-celebrating good humans. A woman who knows the power of her vagina, or anyone tapped into the sheer force of their femininity, will help you celebrate the power of yours. She will throw you a fem-force fiesta if that's what it takes to get you to see that pleasure is power, and that you should wield your force in accordance with your true nature. My girls and I meet each other where we're at. Sexuality advice is always tailored—never one size fits all. Because morality has to fit the Spirit. Advice can range from, *Sweetheart, you need a slut weekend in Barbados* or *You need to get it on in the office supply room by Friday* to, *You need to keep your clothes on for a few months and do a sex-tox* or *You've come so far; don't give it away too soon.*

Loose or focused or somewhere in between, sacred sex moves us closer to our power, not further away from what our hearts truly desire.

Forced freedoms are no more empowering than enforced restrictions. Just because you make free love doesn't mean you're freeing your real power. And the inverse is true, too—just because you're a pure monogamist who likes it missionary style doesn't mean you're puritanical. New Age proselytizing is no better than any other dogma. And peer pressure has no place in spiritual work. Or in your pants. Unless, of course, you really want your peers in your pants.

The best response to the complexities of sexuality meeting our spirituality is to become very clear on what works for you. Body, heart, mind, and Soul.

find out how
powerful
you are

13
POWER TOOLS
More awareness, deeper respect,
less dependency

Gearing up to pare down

MY HOME WAS once full of crystals. My whole life was brimming with them. Enormous stones in my living room. Majestic citrines in my studio. A giant labradorite guarded the entryway. I tucked all kinds of gems into my bra, carried carnelian in my jean pockets to activate my girly parts. I wore super-charged stones set in gold on the appropriate fingers to maximize their desired effects. I put them in soil to help my plants flourish. I slept with stones under my pillow. I gave stones as wedding gifts, birthday presents, "welcome to the team" treats. I was The Crazy Crystal Lady.

Today, there is not a single stone to be found in my home or on my person. Not so much as a tiny baby quartz. Nada. Nothing. No stones. I'll fill you in, but first...

Crystals. Meditation. Flower essences. Essential oils. Sacred geometry. Mudras. Mantras. Incantations. Vision boards...

These are all metaphysical technologies, and like any technology, if you don't know how to use it, your motherboard could get fried. And like most technologies, these tools can be neutral, healing, or destructive—it all depends on who programmed them, who's using them, and how they're being used.

We're buying jade eggs via the internet, and sticking them up our vajay-jays. We're learning to "fire breathe" to rev up our mojo, being taught by people who got certified by people who made up their own mojo certification process. During our women's weekends, we're tracing pentacles in the woods and energizing our crystals in the full moonlight, 'cause it's fun!

On one hand, it's heartening that these modalities and mechanisms are making their way into more people's kitchen cabinets. We're hungry to heal and we're taking matters into our own hands. But...

If we really believe in the capacities of these esoteric tools and practices, then we should be more critical about where and from whom we get them, and how we use them in our lives. Meditation saves. Plant medicine heals. Crystals activate. Power to the woo! And, let's be sincerely reverent and aware, so that we don't do damage when we are trying to heal ourselves and others.

Some of the concoctions and conjuring will be incredibly effective. But not necessarily because they are pure and masterfully dispensed practices—rather, because our belief in them is so intense. If you really really really believe that it will work, it probably will—for a while.

But a belief is not Truth.

Let's look into the New Age toolbox...

Mudras

At their most basic, mudras are sacred hand or body gestures; the name comes from a Sanskrit word meaning "seal," "mark," or "gesture." You've probably done mudras in a yoga or meditation class. Or just recall any illustration of the Buddha seated in lotus position with his index finger touching his thumb to form a circle—that's a mudra.

Think of your hands like a control panel for the rest of your body's energy system. Some say that there are thousands of mudras that can generate tremendous power, and they shouldn't be taught to the uninitiated. Makes sense because our fingertips contain numerous concentrated nerve root endings, and these act as discharge points for free energy. Science backs this up, by the way, and confirms that a concentration of free electrons exists around each of your fingertips. Mudras jumpstart electromagnetic currents within the body, which can alter the way your system functions. They are used for manifesting, clarity, and sometimes for healing physical ailments.

If you take a little bit of medicine, even the wrong kind, it's probably not going to have disastrous effects. Regarding mudras, the sagacious Siri Bahadur put it this way for me: "Most people don't have enough energy to mess themselves up with the inappropriate mudra or the correct one done improperly. It's like if you go to buy an Audi with just fifty bucks, you don't get anywhere." But over time, and with a practitioner's intensity, you could mess with your circuits. How do mudras go wrong? Think: headaches, anxious energy, confusion, feeling imbalanced.

You may not look as yoga-tastic, but the next time you're in class and someone gives you a mudra command, you might want to know the ingredients: its purpose, which lineage it was passed down from, and why they're prescribing it for you. In lieu of that, just place your palms face down on your knees and...*breathe.*

Mantras

My mudra rant applies to mantras, too. Briefly, a mantra is a sacred sound, word, or group of words believed to have psychological and spiritual effects. It's an energetic sound formula. The earliest mantras were composed in Vedic Sanskrit by Hindus in India over three thousand years ago. In Sanskrit, "man" means "to think" and "tra" means "tools" or "instruments," so the literal translation of mantra is "instrument of thought."

There are good reasons that there is secretly held knowledge about certain mantras—some mantras that masters would not dare teach to a novice. There are plenty of meditative methodologies, spells, and esoteric how-tos that have been protected for millennia.

One of my choice contemporary thinkers is Sadhguru. After a series of awakening experiences, he left his business empire in India to become a spiritual teacher. This is how he explains mantras: "When you utter a sound, a form is being created. We can create powerful forms by uttering sounds in certain arrangements. This is the yoga of sound. If you have mastery over the sound you also have mastery over the form that is attached to it." Again, science backs this up. You can feed a sound or vibration into an oscilloscope—an electronic test instrument that measures voltage—and it can be converted to voltage, then displayed.

So be aware of what you're chanting, incanting, and putting into your Spotify. Sounds create realities.

Meditation

Trying to activate the Kundalini because you read a book somewhere is like starting to build a nuclear reactor in your home because you read how to do it on the internet.
- Sadhguru

My mudra and mantra rants also apply to meditation.

I once did a particular kind of meditation over the course of about six months. (All I can tell you is that it involved a *lot of Light*.) I went for it. I craved the high of the Light and I wanted *results*. I pumped up the imagery and gave it all I had. I got results, alright. A golf ball–sized lump started forming on my forehead...the beginning of a unicorn horn, I presumed. I had a feeling that this was: A) not good, and B) related to the fancy mind work that I'd been doing.

Of course, Lady Ninja of the Light texted me the same morning that I noticed the bump forming: "D, I scanned you this morning and there's something happening in your head. You need to stop that meditation immediately." Consider it done. Then she explained. "Too much Light infusion too soon can create tumours," she counselled. Well that got my attention. With guidance, I resumed my practice very slowly, increasing my once-weekly meditation by only a few minutes each time. I lightened up on Lighting up.

Kundalini is our primal energy, it's the stuff of our *consciousness*—it's also referred to as our Shakti. In various spiritual traditions, it's symbolized as a serpent because Kundalini energy lies "coiled" at the base of our spine. In practice, the goal is to bring that energetic current up our spinal system toward our crown and beyond. If we awaken that power source, we illuminate our Souls.

Kundalini is *hot*. Literally and figuratively. And it's making its way into more and more self-help circles. One of my less woo-woo friends recently told me about doing an intense Kundalini breathing and posture exercise, her first of that type of meditation, at a business conference of all places. I raised an eyebrow when she said, "That's some powerful shit! I was so jacked up, I couldn't sleep all night." Uh-huh. I've heard of a woman who didn't sleep for two whole years because of a spontaneous Kundalini awakening. And I don't mean that she had insomnia. I mean she did. not. sleep. for two years straight. She functioned just fine (other than adjusting to the radical psychological stress of the situation) because she was running on that mega cosmic octane.

People who receive a Kundalini energy surge, also referred to as an initiation—either through successful practice or unexpected awakenings—use descriptions like, "My crown opened and it felt like a thousand petals unfolding." "I felt...not separate." "It was like my muscles were orgasming on and off for days." "An overwhelming Love filled me with universal life force." Who doesn't want that? I do! I spend part of every day trying to taste that One Taste.

But you know what can follow an extreme high, especially if it comes unexpectedly? After the waves of bliss, feelings of failure and existential crisis can crash in. Mental instability. Fearfulness. An overwhelming sensation of density and disconnection.

Bonnie Greenwell, PhD, founder of the Kundalini Research Network, speaks with great gravitas about the many teachers of meditation, yoga, and Tantra who are unprepared to handle the confusion that can arise in their students when they have big energy shifts. Even though they are trained practitioners, they have not thoroughly experienced such awakenings for themselves. As Bonnie puts it, "Many students who seek spiritual awakening do not understand the dynamics involved and are not interested in making the major life changes that support the process."

Once you find God/Goddess, He/She may turn your life inside out and you'll be called to reorganize your plans, your mind, and your body. You will finally understand the "work" in "Light worker."

Everything else

So, my rant about mudras and mantras and meditation also applies to everything else.

Like...vision Boards. Yep, they can work. You know it. So shhhh. Maybe keep them to yourself instead of posting your most sacred and visualized desires on Facebook for everybody to project their subconscious opinions on. You might try to keep the details of your dreams just between you and the astral plane so they can marinate in purely positive attention.

And purification rituals. My friend Joshua and I were talking about "cleansing." The juice cleansing, cleansing thought forms, cleansing our space... "Jeezus. When am I cleansed enough already?" he lamented. "Tell me about it," I sighed, sipping on my hot water with lemon, because... cleansing.

Cultures worldwide perform ritual purifications to elevate participants closer to divine purity. I think it's the twenty percent effort of purifying our lives that makes all the difference to our eighty percent of living. A basic analogy: you spend most of your day clothed, put together, and consuming. You spend a relatively small amount of your day on hygiene, preening, and releasing—but without that focused amount of purifying, you and your life would be very unpleasant. We need to cleanse the spirit as much as our body and dwelling spaces.

The problem comes when the cleansing keeps us from living. When we become overly focused on what's dirty and impure, within and without ourselves, we divide the world into good and bad elements. And we miss opportunities to embrace life, to find nourishment in surprising places and build our emotional resiliency.

And psychedelics? Drugs are portals to other dimensions—and like any trip to a foreign land, you just never know what you're going to bring back. Hop on the hallucinogenic highway and you will soon find out that you're not the only one in the fast lane. Other entities and disembodied energies are zooming along right beside you and they might want what you've got: a healthy psyche, Light to spare, and earthly connections.

I've done my share of trips and I wonder if I would have ended up just as "illuminated" if I'd chosen contemplative practices instead. A mushroom trip that I once did in San Francisco sunk me into deep mortal coil for exactly three weeks and I was more than out of sorts. I had to claw my way back to the happiness of being alive again. Was that a useful experience? Sure. Necessary? I think there are other ways to appreciate my mental health.

If you're going to use substances to travel to other realms, please be in good shape for the journey—mentally strong, spiritually fit. Know where your substances are coming from. And don't leave home without a tour guide. But even then, think twice about it.

As for my once-precious crystals...

Every stone has its purpose and its properties for healing and manifestation. Crystals are a programmable technology. And just like they can be engineered to give creative energy, they can be instructed to absorb and redirect it. Programming stones with polluted intention is, amongst virtuous metaphysicians, considered to be an act that comes with serious karmic consequences. It's not only an abuse of power, but a desecration of the mineral kingdom.

A seasoned and feisty practitioner once gave me this food for thought: "Everyone knows you can buy a stone in Bali from a witch doctor for seven U.S. dollars that will curse your mother-in-law. By the time you get home, the spell is in full effect and the old lady's fallen ill." Actually, not everyone knows that. Many of us might just think stones are beautiful and potentially mystical. "So unless you trip over a crystal popping out of the earth, leave them where they are!" she advised. Got it. Sadhguru is equally pragmatic on the topic of crystals: "Stones can wreak havoc in people's lives because they don't know how to use them." Don't I know it.

I know it because you could say I had a *run-in* with one of the maligned healers that the real-deal healers warn us about. Letting an ill-intentioned energy worker into your life and energy field is like giving an embezzler the password to your online bank accounts—they move the money around to make it look like they're being helpful, but with every transaction, they're siphoning some for themselves. It's all very exciting until you wake up drained and confused.

I worked with this person professionally for many months and it created an unbelievable amount of chaos in my life. It wasn't quite as dramatic as Harry Potter's saga with *He-Who-Must-Not-Be-Named*—but in my Muggle reality, it came close. It's as juicy and bizarre as you might imagine: months of sleep disturbances, projectile vomiting for no apparent reason, throbbing solar plexus pain, startling dreams and visions, and things that go bump in the night.

When that healer-client relationship started to unravel, a number of other cosmic advisors started showing up in my life, like knights stepping out of the mists to come to my rescue. A friend's trusted seer had a portentous dream about the situation and rang her to pass on a message to me: *Tell her she must remove the stones from her house.* I was referred to a medicine man in the southwest who was already praying for me when he received my first call. *Remove the stones from your house*, he advised. Yet another friend's go-to healer reached out to me and passionately urged me to *remove the stones*. "This is serious, Danielle. If you don't get those crystals out of your house," she implored, "I'm going to get on a plane and do it for you."

You know what I did? I disappeared those stones. It wasn't easy, emotionally or otherwise. It took tremendous support and metaphysical rigour but the crystals and a lot of other things in my life got put into new order. All of the metaphysical kung fu that the "healer" taught me to use became part of my own skilled defense system. It took a few months, but all of the malevolent mayhem went on back where it came from.

It was a fantastic initiation in the power of Light. And dark. You can't have one without the other.

But if you insist...

> *I have had my glimpses with and without substances*
> *I have had awakenings non-abiding for the most part*
> *And here we go out here on the edge of evolution*
> *Numbers growing out here on the edge of evolution*
> - Alanis Morissette, "Edge of Evolution"

All the tools and promises for feeling better, for being more powerful—they're *irresistible*. The highs, the specialness, the deliverance from pain, the future foretold, the backstage pass to reality. We want it. Hoarding metaphysical tools can give us a sense of control and power, but we need to check that we're not using them as shortcuts to what we need to learn to do on our own—what we *can* do on our own.

And while we're looking at our strength in relation to our growth, we should be analyzing the class society that's been born of the wellness movement. Being active in the wellness scene has become a subtle status symbol. The team directory of most yoga studios and course sites is stocked with predominantly white, slim, and well-accessorized people. It's not because holistic folk are exclusionary, it's partly a matter of economics. We have to be aware that it takes some social privilege to access all of the accoutrements of a New Age lifestyle. Yoga classes in my city average $18 each. The best green juice in town is $10 a bottle. Some pricey medicinal herbs are sold by companies that exploit the workers who harvest them. The cost of organic produce, not to mention having easy access to it in small towns and urban centres (google "food desert" for some perspective)...it's out of reach for too many people. I'm asking myself these days, at the end of a yoga class, when I'm slamming down a green protein shake and feeling really and truly grateful, *How can we turn these blessings into the basics for everyone?*

Should we avoid esoteric practices and teachers altogether and take the path of total self-reliance? We can't. And we shouldn't—this is part of our awakening. What we should do, at many stops along the way, is recommit to our spiritual education. We should scrutinize every class, every sermon, every theory, with the respect that our Soul—and our greatest teachers—deserve.

For me, less is more. The less spiritual paraphernalia I have in my life, the more clarity I can access. No crutches, more strength. I do more homework than I've ever done before. And I've curbed my dependency on all of it—the tinctures, the teachers, the stones.

Goodbye power tools, hello power.

worship what
you love &
love the
way you
worship

14

THE PATH WITHIN YOUR PATH

The roundabout journey
to life-affirming discipline

"MEDITATOR" ISN'T A label I'd give myself, though I've meditated for years—in temples, on the bus, on cushions, in the tub, with and without mala beads and rosaries and formalities and instructors. Some of my best meditations have happened on the rowing machine at my community centre, eyes closed and my "I Like to Move It" playlist getting me higher and hotter.

Meditation, contemplation, visualization. Guided imagery. Prayer. As terms and practices, these are all interchangeable, unique, and, understandably, misunderstood. People who put things like "Joe has been a meditator for twenty years" in their bios always make me wonder. If you're an actual meditation teacher, of course that would be a resumé essential. But otherwise...well, just because you're a formal meditator doesn't mean you're not an asshole. Meditating doesn't ensure that you'll be more considerate or easy to get along with; it just means that you can call yourself a meditator. But ya...I'm a meditator.

In my twenties, I was trying on vipassana meditation at the 7:00 p.m. class at a Buddhist meditation centre in Seattle. After a few weeks of sessions, the instructor asked how it was going for me. "You know, my mind feels emptier, and I suppose that's good, because you say it is. But..." I admitted sheepishly, not quite recognizing my own wisdom at the time, "my heart feels dry."

For a long time, my contemplative practice was active prayer. And in my conversational prayers with Christ, I felt a golden warmth in my heart. Relating to Him stirred my honey-heartedness, my greatest affection for life itself.

I would struggle in the space between mental discipline and emotional nourishment, the intellect and the spirit, for a long time. Often, I got stuck in my head and would judge myself for craving the comforts of a fuller heart. I tried to think my way through spontaneity. I prayed for meditation to be easier. My relationship to prayer and meditation has been a mottled mess that turned into a work of art, once I stepped back to see it more clearly.

At one point, I stopped formally meditating. Intentionally. Not like when you don't go to the gym one week and then a month goes by. I just made a declaration to hang up my mala beads and call it quits for an indefinite period of time.

The very thing I was doing to feel liberated felt confining. My practice, which was not that gruelling to begin with since I never sat for hours at a time, started to feel like one more thing *to do*. I had to drag myself to it. Meditation had become an assignment, and I felt like I was being graded by an invisible monk in the sky, who probably sat next to the man in robes that I imagined God to be for the longest time. It was becoming a way to reinforce my "goodness"—good at taking care of myself, at seeking, at being holistic—good at being good. And meditation was becoming a stimulant for being "on." Meditate before the gig, before the interview, before the meeting to make sure I was on top of it. It was like caffeine for performing, which isn't necessarily a bad thing. But I was getting nervous that I couldn't function optimally without it. I was anxious about meditating—which I was pretty sure was not the goal of having a meditation practice.

From this frustration, a question surfaced: how present could I be if I didn't *prepare to be present*? I dared myself.

I just got out of bed in the morning and started my day. No pressure to make time to contemplate. It was a bit of a rebellious rush, a reprieve. And I didn't fall apart without meditation. I still had lots of creative ideas, misery didn't creep up on me, my comedic timing was still fucking *excellent*.

My dear shrink, Michael B., is a long-time meditator and devout Buddhist (but he would never say that on his bio). I was about six months into my ommmm-free zone and was really eager to ask him, "Why do you meditate?" I was expecting a profound response along the lines of, "to free myself from afflictive states," or "to enter into non-dualistic awareness." But he just shrugged and said, "It's comforting." That was revelatory for me. *Comforting.*

And soon after, meditation and me...we *so* got back together. On new terms that worked for both of us. I gave myself permission to relate to the practice in the way that was easiest and most pleasurable. What a concept.

I meditate for clarity. I meditate to manifest what I desire. I meditate to be of service. (And when my meditation is an act of loving and healing others, I get much more ecstatic, much faster. I Love how that works.) I meditate because I deeply crave communion with The Mother of All Things, The Spaciousness That Cradles. I meditate because it feels good and I want to feel *that good* as much as possible. *Comforting.*

Meditation, yoga, eating clean

I've had similar push-pull-despise-adore relationships with meditation, yoga, and clean eating. Curious and resistant. Then resistance melts into affection, then affection turns into commitment. I've learned to follow the pull, rather than obey the push.

I had to break away from each of these paths to come back to them on my own terms. I had to do the dance of "I don't need you, but I want you." I proved to myself that I'm okay without the mantras, I can function just fine without the asanas, and gluten and dairy didn't kill me. But I want more than "okay" and "fine" and "not dead." I want radiance, and I want to use that radiance to serve.

If we can agree that some form of contemplation, moving your body, and healthy eating is actually a spiritual calling, then here are a few thoughts on going prodigal and coming home to practice.

Identify where you are already meeting with Spirit in your life. A lot of us have regular habits that bring us closer to the Light. We should declare those for what they are: our spiritual rituals. That quiet moment you give yourself before you head in to a meeting—communing with your higher guidance. Girl time at your place with hummus and olives and laughs—like women have been gathering in tents and temples for millennia. Working in the garden—serving the Earth.

It's important what you call your practice. Maybe you're not a "meditator," but every morning you read scriptures with your Earl Grey tea, or you write in your journal. That's a contemplative practice. Call it that and keep doing it. Maybe, much like myself, you resist the meditator label but you actually *do* meditate regularly—just admit it, you're a modest meditator (and don't ever put it on your bio). Is prayer more your style? Then call it a prayer practice, because it is.

There is no competition. I've been doing yoga on and off for twenty years and I've never attended an advanced level class—not because I've progressed so far on my own but because I'm a perma-beginner. (Actually, I did end up in an advanced class one night because I misread the schedule. It could have been humiliating but instead I let it be hilarious...because it was so humiliating.) I may go months with only doing a few poses in my office every morning, and then I'll dive in again with regular classes. My only aspiration is to let it be a gentle and abiding practice in my life.

No one else can quantify the value of your practice for you. You may get more out of a one-time silent retreat than another practitioner gleans in months of meditation. One sincere prayer could be as effective for you as hours of prostrations.

Remember, it's about ongoing practice, not permanence. One of Jiddu Krishnamurti's students said to him, "I find it impossible to be aware all the time." His reply: "Don't be aware all the time. Just be aware in little bits."

Even with steady devotion to your growth, your practices will ebb and flow. Some days you're going to be riding high, dancing to merge with Shiva himself, or fasting to feel the pulse of the higher realms. Other days, you're just doing what it takes not to feel like shit.

Be *your* kind of devotee, *your* kind of Light chaser.

Worship what you Love and Love the way you worship.

Have an
opinion.
Use it.

15

DISCERNMENT
IS EVERYTHING
When the negative serves the positive

My new life in golden

After I learned how to breathe under water
I knew that my lungs had all the answers

My skills in courage were as follows:
swallowing terror whole
making good use of disgust
boring a hole in the kitchen floor with my tears
loving like what I Loved was the only child ever to be
born of the sun and moon
changing my mind while naked
breaking vows
making a new vow (only one)
leaning back and taking deeply deep breaths of space
watching the Universe reveal all of us to me.

my reward is as follows:
I get to go wherever I want now and always,
for instance,
under water or
to that golden spot that I thought was only a dream
but is now my New Life breathing me.

We must always take sides. Neutrality helps the oppressor, never
the victim. Silence encourages the tormentor, never the tormented...
There may be times when we are powerless to prevent injustice,
but there must never be a time when we fail to protest.

– Elie Wiesel, Nobel Peace Prize acceptance speech, 1986

I RARELY SAY ANYTHING overtly critical on my social media channels. If I see a movie that I didn't like or read a book that was only half good, I just don't mention it. Everybody has their art and their living to make. If you don't have anything nice to say...don't tweet about it. On the other hand, if I come across something that I'm wild about, I buzz it up. Generally, I try to keep all of my communication positive. Because every word is energy and there's too much reactive aggression happening on every platform—digital and literal. Because, good manners. Because Love.

Keeping it "positive" does not preclude having strong opinions. When I think my opinions might inspire some awareness and action, then I'll mouth off. And that's an almost daily occurrence. I'm mouthy. When I go at an issue, I'm as considerate as I can be, especially if there are individuals rather than a corporate brand involved. Being offensive and polarizing is inevitable if you have opinions, but you can have an opinion and keep it kind.

Sometimes, you have to go right to the heart of an issue and call people on their bullshit-making—which might not seem like a very "spiritual" thing to do. But let me tell you...opinions used for raising standards are sacred indeed. At times, being a Light worker means you keep your heart aglow with compassion. And on other occasions, you will have to use your Truth like a lightsaber and take some bullshit down.

Being discerning is not the same as being judgmental. Discernment is big-minded and awake. Judgment is narrow-minded and operates in the dark. Discernment is our wisdom coming to life.

Judgment is nasty any way you slice it. It's divisive and reactionary and very unaccommodating. It has a limited perspective, a pinched face, and a heart that closes by default. It gets easily confused because it's only looking in one direction. Judgment works really hard to camouflage feeling threatened. It's very "me" versus "other." It says "but" a lot. *But I... but you...but I...but you...*

Discernment, on the other hand, looks at the bigger picture to make sense of what's going on. It takes a number of details into account and measures them against its sense of right and wrong—in the moment. Discernment isn't easily swayed, because it has a strong sense of self. That rootedness allows it to be more flexible. Without the power of discernment, you'll fall for anything, you'll abandon yourself, and all kinds of harmful lies and agendas can seep into your life.

> If harmony at any cost is revered as the sole spiritual aim, then discernment is often unwelcome. But if Truth is the aspiration, then discernment is a heroine.

The few times I've publicly called out individuals for their less-than-luminous lifestyles or behaviours, I've gotten this pushback: *Well, that's being awfully judgmental, don't you think? We need to support each other. There's room for everybody.* But actually, in my personal life, there is *not* room for everyone. Not at all. Some ideologies are categorically damaging to the human spirit and I feel honour-bound to point them out, for my civil liberties and collective justice, for my child's future, for the Light I might spark with just one voiced opinion. Is this righteous? Most definitely.

Knowing what's right and what's wrong for you doesn't mean that you're judgmental—it's called being in touch with your Higher Power. And you should let your Higher Power mouth off for the greater good.

Fight with Light

You can't have the Light without the dark. It's a primary function of metaphysical teachers to emphasize the power of the Light, but they can neglect to address the realities of dealing with the darkness. I was at an angel workshop (don't judge me), and a woman who was mentioning some government conspiracy theories was hushed by the workshop leader. "We can't talk about negative things like that, it gives it energy." Please, if you can't talk about whacky conspiracy theories at an angel reading workshop, then where can you talk about them?

Every Light bearer will, at some point, have to get wise to the dark. Just ask the Archangel Michael. He's the angel of supreme protection, one of the most prevalent and popular angels in contemporary spiritual teachings.

If you do some art history homework on the Archangel Michael, you'll notice a big difference between how Christian Renaissance artists and today's illustrators portray him. Pull from any modern angel deck and Michael is a muscular warrior, standing (or flying) solo with a radiant electric-blue sword or massive wings. He's a total celestial stud. I really do Love these portrayals. But something's missing that the past depictions typically feature: the demons that Michael is slaying. Older paintings show Michael spearing gnarly gargoyle creatures or monstrous men of war. He is taking the darkness *down*. Dude's on a mission. The Catholic Prayer to St. Michael the Archangel reads, "Be our protection...by the divine power, thrust into hell Satan and all evil spirits who prowl about the world, seeking the ruin of souls. Amen." Subtle. This makes the Archangel Michael affirmations you'll find in modern metaphysical shops look like nursery rhymes. Michael's gotten awfully subdued these days. New Age–washed, as it were.

But we live in a world with problems much more complex than nursery rhymes. There is darkness and negativity that needs to be faced and dealt with from the micro to the macro levels of society. And I want an army of warrior angels to have my back and to be prepared to slay. I want to see depravity where it is, keep an eye on it, and *then* deliberately choose to work for the Light with every single thought and deed. Every day.

The divine utility of disgust

We must recognize the incorrect situation for what it is and carefully keep disengaged from it. This is to judge it without allowing our attitude to become judgmental. In such situations we need help from a Higher Power. Awareness of this need enables us to keep balance "on the high wire," as it were, for that is what is required.

– Carol K. Anthony, *A Guide to The I Ching*

An ally of discernment—and one of the rougher, least-promoted emotions in spiritual circles—is disgust. We're taught, for the sake of politeness, not to fully experience, let alone express, our disgust. It's labelled as a negative emotion because, well, *it is* a negative emotion. It's potentially dehumanizing if used against someone else, and its buildup can be poison to our psyches. And, it can be an incredibly effective tool for mindfulness. In the Pixar movie *Inside Out*, they did a brilliant job of defining the value of the character "Disgust." They say, "It's Disgust's job to keep Riley [the main character] from being poisoned—physically or socially." Disgust is like the spit-out function of both our bodies and Souls—life-saving though not so glamorous.

After ongoing disagreements with someone in my life, things finally erupted and I needed to get untangled and figure out how to proceed. I was working with an intuitive healer on the situation. She was a calm and centred personality, firm but infinitely patient. I was expecting her to prescribe an exercise for self-Love or cutting energetic cords—something esoteric. But instead, she said to me, like a ship's captain in the midst of a squall, "You need to use your disgust. Let yourself be absolutely, fully, completely disgusted by the ordeal." *So no...affirmations of divine Love? Just...go disgusto on the whole thing?*

I worried for a minute that my "disgust vibe" was going to turn toxic on me. I didn't want to send heaps of negativity to the other party involved, either. What I did want was to protect myself from their antics. I looked at their morals, I looked at mine, and there was no doubt: I was disgusted by the contrast.

So I went with it. When I thought of the situation, as was my some-times healthy habit, I'd start to feel sympathy for the other party involved, and then I'd start thinking about ways I could be more accommodating, and then I'd end up frustrated and unclear. So I looked at the ordeal internally and very matter-of-factly said, *You disgust me.* At first I laughed at myself because it felt uncomfortably dramatic, *Like, that's a little intense.* But it only took one or two more rounds to feel the Truth of what I was stating: that I *was* disgusted. Thoroughly. And therefore, things could not go on as they had.

It was a healthy defense at the time, and it gave me strength to put new rules in place for myself. As Robert Augustus Masters describes healthy disgust, "It defends us against impurity, real or imagined... Healthy disgust doesn't degrade others. It focuses on *behaviours* that we find repugnant, giving us the impetus to so strongly reject such behaviours that we unmistakably stand apart from them while simultaneously standing in our integrity." *Discerned.*

Call bullshit when you need to—and keep it classy. The Golden Rule applies. (When doesn't it?) *Do unto others as you would have them do unto you*—even if you want nothing to do with them.

There were times in the past (and I'm sure some wait for me in the future, too) when I was harsh and less than deeply considerate when standing up for my opinions. I was striving and I was stressed, and I decided to pretend that I didn't know that energy turns into matter, can hurt people, and can come back to hurt me.

There's always a way to be elegant, no matter whose side you're on—but first, you need to know where you stand. Take your place. And have your lightsaber in reach.

Ask your
Soul
what it
sees

16
REGARDING SUFFERING
Soul, pain, perspective

Permission to suffer

I am emboldened by the puzzling and redemptive truth...
we are made by what would break us.
– Krista Tippett, *Becoming Wise*

B EFORE WE DIG in, let me lay down a core theory, which we'll circle back to: pain and suffering are two different experiences. Pain is the result of an event that hurt you. You break up with someone, you feel pain. You break a bone, you feel pain. Pain is always the first response to being hurt.

Suffering is your response to the pain. Pain in life is inevitable. Suffering, however, is somewhat more...*optional.*

Hold that thought.

Here's a commonly held spiritual premise: pain and suffering are our teachers. True.

Ergo, the New Age follow-up: since pain and suffering are our teachers, we should be *grateful* for our pain and suffering.

Um...not so fast.

Let's talk about the shame of suffering. It's a New Age specialty; we self-helpers are experts at criticizing ourselves for manifesting, attracting, and then having a less-than-Zen response to tough times.

If we regard pain as a learning opportunity when at the same time we're drowning in sorrow and wondering "Why me?!" then we might feel a bit dim. *After all the meditation, and therapy, and reiki, I mean, you'd think I could get over this...*

When the person you want doesn't want you, when you didn't get the gig that you hustled so hard to get, when there's a diagnosis, when you suffer a near-unspeakable loss, and/or/but... You've been working soooo long for a breakthrough, then your "inner winner" might sound like this: *Fuck "everything happens for a reason." Fuck the "Divine Plan."* And while we're at it, *Fuck all you power-of-positive-thinking people!*

Pain is pain. Loss is loss. Abuse is abuse. Suffering is suffering.

As spiritual as it may appear, gratitude is not always the best initial response to a challenge. Our suffering doesn't want to be denied or talked down to with spiritually correct platitudes. It wants our attention—it's screaming for it. When we paint over pain with premature positivity, we short circuit our healing. And that kind of avoidance actually makes us more susceptible to future wounding. It's why the lesson keeps coming back. Maybe we should hold off on the spiritual sweetener, experience our genuine reaction to the upsetting event, and go from there.

First, you cleanse a wound—which usually stings like a muther. Then you dress and bandage it—which is much more comforting. When all is not well in your world, be right there—where the wound happened. Be hurt, be furious, be weak. Be where it's ugly and uncomfortable. Hold off on the karmic explanations, the family of origin connections, and the "it's all good" equalizers—those balms and bandages can come later.

The spiritual response to suffering is to befriend it. If your friend were in pain, you wouldn't tell her to be thankful for the learning. If she showed up crying, you wouldn't scowl and say, "*You* again?" or rush her out the door. You'd sit down with your suffering friend and let her vent. Or maybe you wouldn't need to exchange words; just being quiet would be restorative. You'd take your friend and her agony out to the movies. And you'd Love her for being so real with you. And healing would begin.

What *exactly* to be grateful for

I am not grateful for being ousted from a company that I co-founded. I am not grateful for losing $90,000 on a business idea gone south. I am not thankful for the Spirit-crushing ramifications of one particular relationship. And I really could have done without that two-year bout of a mystery illness. There have been losses. And trials that wore me down until I begged for a break.

But holy hell, am I profoundly **grateful for everything that I learned** from those challenges. I'm with Maya Angelou: "Wouldn't take nothing for my journey now." I would not turn back the clock, or take back one tear, tremor, or dollar. All those moments that I had to quell the adrenaline with the power of my mind, or carry buckets of integrity back from the well when I thought it might be dry—that was some serious training. All those revelations of responsibility! So many illusions that got burned *down*! The flames that scarred me are the flames that purified and lifted me up—because I gave myself over to the fire, willing to learn, wanting to know. I got down on my knees, peered under the clouds of smoke and fear, and said, "Let me see what's *really* going on here."

And when I thank Life for what those challenges provided me with, I say, *Thank you for helping me see clearly.* For helping me see where I can grow and how I can get there. Thank you for helping me see where Love is and where fear lurks, and where the Truth has always been.

> There's no need to be grateful for your hardships and for the perpetrators themselves. Because, remember: the Universe brings you more of what you are grateful for. So be grateful for the Faith and the friends that held you when it all fell apart.

> Be grateful that you have the capacity to transform suffering into learning, and brokenness into resilience. Be grateful for your strength to handle the challenge.

Sicka it

My home girl, Piper, texted me to say she broke her foot. I went into warp speed analysis of the critical situation.

Me: What!? You broke it? That blows. You in pain?
Piper: I was, but the painkillers are rad. Warm and fuzzy.

And with that effort of compassion out of the way, I got all metaphysical on her physical.

Me: Which foot?
Piper: Left.
Me: The feminine side. How'd you do it?
Piper: Tripped over Felix's hockey bag.
Me: So he's blocking your forward movement. OBVIOUSLY. Where were you going?
Piper: Downstairs.
Me: Descending into the subconscious.
Piper: I'm so sick of tripping on his shit.
Me: Word.

Clearly this meant that Piper had to break up with Felix because his Neanderthal ways were impeding her full expression of her life's purpose. *Clearly.* Now, metaphysically speaking, Piper and I were in sync with the assessment. But maybe what my friend also needed at that time was some chicken soup and for me to pick up her mail. Less scrutiny, more TLC.

I've been on the other side of that insta-analysis. I dealt with chronic bronchial infections for years. (I was so ashamed of how recurring it was. Why couldn't I heal myself?) And if I ever mentioned it to holistic-type folk, they'd lean closer to me and say, as if they were giving me the cure to the plague, "Lungs are about grief." *Oh really? Thanks so much. Because I haven't already talked to ninety psychic naturopaths about this.*

We New Agers Love to analyze the shit out of our somatic, embodied everything. And yes, the Soul does speak through the body, but there's a potentially massive pitfall to this chronic analysis. What if our illness can't be easily explained or corroborated with a spiritual lesson? What if it feels impossible to emotionally and spiritually reckon with? What if, as much as we try...we *can't* heal ourselves?

To someone who's spent years strengthening their mind-body connection, illness can hit the Spirit hard. *How could I have manifested this? What am I clinging to on a cellular level?* In spite of all the work we do to transcend, physical illness brings us back down to earth to tend to our breath and bones—it renders us more human than ever. In one of Oprah's SuperSoul Sessions I attended, Caroline Myss spoke right to this: "Illness hits and we think that we are the exception to the rule. That's one of the most painful things you can tell yourself—that you're above the laws of nature." We are part of nature animating itself. Life-giving, diseased, restorative—all of it.

Many powerful gurus with the capacity to heal other people have died of common types of cancer and organ failure. The mystic Jiddu Krishnamurti (who, incidentally, is my biggest philosopher crush) suffered wretched migraines later in his life before he died. Both the Buddhist monk Thích Nhất Hạnh and spiritual teacher Ram Dass have suffered debilitating strokes. About his illness, Dass wrote, "All my life I had been a 'helper.' I now found myself forced to accept the help of others, and to admit that my body needed attention." He added, "Recently, a friend said to me, 'You're more human since the stroke than you were before.' This touched me profoundly. What a gift the stroke has given me, to finally learn that I don't have to renounce my humanity in order to be spiritual—that I can be both witness and participant, both eternal spirit and aging body."

The body is a vehicle for the Soul, and the Soul is in the driver's seat.

Sometimes illness is a dramatic wake-up call. The Soul is trying desperately to get the attention of the personality that's so caught up in the materialist world that they've forgotten their true Nature. Illness can deliver the message you need to get into balance. *Your Spirit is hurting. Slow down. Take charge. Surrender. Feel the greater connection.*

And sometimes, illness might be an initiation into our greater healing capacities, schooling in manipulating matter with our minds. Maybe we signed up to learn about cycles of time and patience. Maybe illness shows up so we can serve others with our hard-won knowledge of what it takes to be more fully alive. Maybe we're releasing karma, or we're serving others by processing a collective pain. Maybe we're learning to co-exist with the mystery of it all—which is a monumental lesson.

All for Soul

> *I believe in deeply ordered chaos.*
> – Francis Bacon

I believe that, from the Soul level, we choose our pain.

This is interconnected with a foundational belief that I have: that our Souls travel through multiverses in multitudinous forms and dimensions; more simply put, we experience many incarnations. So I don't subscribe to an idea of a spiritual lottery or a dictator-god-force dispensing destinies or favouritism. I think that we, as human sparks of the pure Life Source, set out to have as many experiences as necessary to return to our wholeness. We work in tandem with Creation to choose each life's general circumstances, penciling in the lesson plan and signing a few contracts before we incarnate. We choose our roles in the theatre of life: the victim, the vanquisher, the crusader, the lover. The hermit, the leader, the fool, the sage.

And some human lives are just easier or harder than others. Some are more effective in developing knowledge and skill. It's all chosen. It's all useful. It's all helpful in expanding the Universe.

So it would follow that we, our limitless Souls, even choose to experience horrific abuses and debilitating losses—the kinds of things that we may never recover from in just one human lifetime. We also choose grace and every kind of incredible fortune and blissful blessing. We are dark and Light. Eventually, in time infinitum, we will have sampled and feasted from everything on the cosmic menu.

Does this "Soul point of view" of choosing my pain prevent me from actually feeling pain? Of course not. When my heart is broken, or I feel humiliation, or anxiety, or attacked—it's painful. When the people dearest to me are in pain, I feel their pain. I feel humanity's pain. I hurt deeply and frequently, even more so as I feel our interconnectedness more every day. And I suffer over my pain. It slows me down, it fogs my clarity, and the frustration can make me lash out inwardly and outwardly. I have begged for my Soul to know better, for my guides to deliver me from each hard lesson, for the Mother and the Father to have mercy on my Soul.

Does this Soul point of view help to ease my *suffering*? Does it mitigate my negative response to the pain? Yes. Sometimes this perspective helps me *immensely*. Other times, just barely. I see meaningfulness in most things and I take comfort in my belief that Soul growth is always being made.

Does believing that my Soul sanctioned the most painful experiences of my life—from being an innocent child to a mature adult—mean that I think I "deserved" to have those bad things happen to me? Not at all, not whatsoever. We all deserve protection and care and respect. When anyone is victimized or burdened in any way, the highest response is unbridled compassion.

Do I think that when something negative happens to me or in my life that I brought it on myself? Sure, sometimes. I'm creating huge parts of my reality—in tandem with my Soul and God/Goddess. And there are always so many factors co-working and co-conspiring. The reasons for a negative event may never be clear to me from my human perspective.

Do I think negative events are a punishment? Never, ever, ever. I think I work in concert with Life to challenge myself, and "punishment" doesn't go where Love is. I do not believe in a wrathful god consciousness. That said, hardship can feel incredibly punishing and there have been many times that I spoke to Life and pleaded, "You've *got* to be kidding me."

Does any of this mean that I passively accept misfortune, poor treatment, or let any perpetrators of harm off the hook because I feel complicit in some way? Not a chance. My connection to the wisdom of my Soul informs my self-worth. It supports me to dispel darkness with the intelligence of Love, and pursue a justice that heals.

Does my Soul perspective block my human self-compassion? It can. As you hear in most every chapter, my lack of self-compassion on my path was an impetus for writing *White Hot Truth*. My struggle to reconcile my spiritual viewpoint with my human desires is ongoing—and totally thrilling. The journey tests me often, but I am resolved never to turn my back on my Soul.

...

The social critic and comedian Stephen Colbert was asked about how he made sense of the great loss in his life. When he was ten years old, his father and two brothers died in a plane crash. When he asked his mom, a devout Catholic, how God could do such a horrible thing, she counselled him to *"see it with the perspective of eternity."* This is the Soul's point of view. "And by her example I am not bitter," Colbert said.

This is how I've made meaning out of the world we live in: I believe our Soul is guiding us through every kind of experience. And I'm learning to be at ease with how unfathomable that is.

Extremes & exceptions

> *Between stimulus and response there is a space. In*
> *that space lies our power to choose our response. In*
> *our response lies our growth and our freedom.*
> – Viktor E. Frankl, *Man's Search For Meaning*

A critical mind will ask, *Okay, so if someone decided to incarnate into a refugee camp, or to be born with the Zika virus, how is that person going to rise above that kind of extreme suffering?* Excellent question.

I don't think anyone "rises above" extreme suffering while they're actually in it. They are surviving, wrestling to hold on to their sanity or life. Some people can find glimmers of Light within overwhelming darkness. Like Viktor Frankl, who found the will to live through three years in concentration camps in Nazi Germany by finding personal meaning in the experience. "Those who have a 'why' to live, can bear with almost any 'how,'" he wrote. Nelson Mandela, imprisoned for twenty-seven years before serving as president of South Africa, worked to keep his vision of the future alive. "I always knew that someday I would once again feel the grass under my feet and walk in the sunshine as a free man."

Survivors of atrocity are astounding for staying alive, and sane. And what's even more stunning is what some people do after they are emancipated: they forgive. With every right to be bitter and retaliative, they choose to preach and practice Love. They find joy. They still believe in a just God. These are *exceptional* humans. Nobel Laureate Elie Wiesel said, "That I survived the Holocaust and went on to love beautiful girls, to talk, to write, to have toast and tea and live my life—that is what is abnormal." *Exceptional.*

How one Soul maps out its requirements for growth—through pain or pleasure, ease or hardship—is unique, inexplicable, and entirely unknowable from an Earth-bound perspective. The playing field called "Earth" is not level for everyone. This is exactly why some motivational self-help sermons do us an injustice. Not everyone can "achieve it if they just believe it." And to apply that theory over everyone with broad strokes is degrading to those in extreme situations of oppression, disenfranchisement, and disability.

Some of us will rise above the suffering in a given lifetime. Some of us will not. There is no way to make the human struggle "comfortable." And becoming comfortable with it isn't the point.

No pity for a strong Soul

For two years, at nearly the same time every weekday, I would hear unintelligible yelling directly in front of my house, right outside the window I faced while writing. It was a groaning, a holler of utterances and yelps—maybe pain, maybe a secret code, maybe joy trying to unmute itself. It was impossible to ignore.

The noises came from a guy in his twenties who always wore white sneakers and a red rain jacket, with shorn brown hair and big brown eyes. I presumed he had a severe form of cerebral palsy or brain damage. His hands were balled up in fists, held up close to his handsome but always contorted face. His head was cocked sideways and upward. And when he would holler, which was almost constantly, it looked as if he was communicating with Spirits at the tops of the trees.

In my mind, I called him Jerry. He always walked down my side of the street with his very laid-back caregiver a few feet ahead of him. She strolled. Jerry just...hollered. I had guests over one afternoon when he limped-dragged-walked by, hollering, LOUDLY. They looked alarmed and rushed to the front window. "What the...?"

It's Jerry. He hollers.

My heart broke every time he came by. I thought mostly of all the things he'd never do. He'd never hold a pen and sign a cheque. Or make steamed rice and eat it with friends, talking about politics and deals on flights. Or read a book in the bathtub. Or ride a motorcycle with his sweetheart on the back of it. Not this lifetime.

For the first few weeks when Jerry walked by, I'd go into the kitchen to make tea because I just couldn't bear to watch. And then I remembered something my mom said to me when I was a little girl. We saw a very gnarled man in a wheelchair, painstakingly making his way across the street. My mom noticed the angsty concern on my face.

"Strong Soul," she said, as we waited on the corner. "People like him have Souls that can take it."

Believing her words didn't take away the pain I felt, and I'm not sure if it would have comforted the man in the wheelchair either. But it dissolved my pity—and made room for the most immense kind of respect. Now when I witness suffering, one of my internal responses to that person is reverence. *You're an incredible being for taking this on.*

I came to look forward to Jerry's afternoon strolls. The louder, the better. And I'm sure that Jerry, the strong Soul that he is, looked up at the trees, and through Life, and saw all sorts of things that I did not.

Suffering to service

When the suffering is almost intolerable. When you've had all you think you can take. When you can't comprehend what the gift in the pain might be. When "making progress" is painful to consider...

There's this:

May my suffering be of service.
At the very least.
May some good come of this.
If not for me, for someone else.
Some good.
At the very least.
May my suffering be of service.

It's a sublime Buddhist approach to pain. When you're in hell, the notion that your agony might have some divine utility can help you endure. It's a Light ray of reason, a thread of meaning that you can grab onto in deep confusion.

Your pain and suffering are of service. When you're on the other side of it, your I've-been-through-it wisdom is going to comfort someone else, perhaps many people, profoundly. And when you're in the real-time agony, it's a contribution even then. You are burning energetic pathways. You're clearing space, and rectifying, and learning—you're coming to know your Soul.

It's a prayer, really:
May my suffering be of service.

Energy
follows
thought

17
DESIRE, REFINED
A broader view for creating reality

Dear Infinity

soon
enough
My Future
will be
now
and my scars will have grown into
sacred geometry
(circles of Dignity, pyramids of Will, vortices of Love)

I hide what I had to let go of in furrows
behind a tall gate
and I whisper wishes
into each victory seed
I plant —
every one hears this prayer:

Dear Infinity,
Breathe life into
my every desire.

Perspectives on desire

The Catholics: If you want it, you have to go through God to get it.
The Buddhists: Your problem is that you want it.
The Zen Buddhists: What's to want?
The Hindus: You wanted that in your last life.
The Capitalists: You gotta want it more than anyone else.
The New Agers: Just keep telling the Universe how much you want it.

EVERYBODY WANTS WHAT they want, but New Agers in particular set out to *manifest and co-create* and master the universal secrets of getting what they want. We are all up in the Goddess' grill when it comes to wanting to know the principles of manifestation, the laws of attraction, and the science of desire.

Some of the manifestation teachings that have become popular have done us a bit of a disservice. They skew heavily toward *getting* what you want instead of *being what you want*. So much *getting* keeps us in the materialist trap, and we're never going to find satisfaction there.

Do you think a workshop called, "Manifest Your Life Desires: Your Chances Are 50/50" would sell tickets? Nah. But it would be honest. It's a rare manifestation course that addresses what happens when you *don't* actually manifest what you want, which is often the case because...life. And karma. And lack of clarity. And your Soul may have other plans for you.

And too often, desired **feelings** aren't even part of the manifestation equation—which is a total miss. Because we're not actually chasing the goal; we're chasing how we want to feel when we reach it. If you're not clear on how you want to feel, you'll keep running in law-of-attraction circles. *Got the promotion, still feel unseen. Got the relationship, still have abandonment issues. Got the house, still don't feel at home.* Intentional creating boils down to what I call your Core Desired Feelings. Once you get clear on those, *then* you'll know what you *really* want, and you can set about doing whatever generates your Core Desired Feelings. It's not so much about attainment—it's about *attunement* with your heart and Soul.

I've done *beaucoup* research on the art and science of manifestation. I even wrote a book about it—*The Desire Map*—and built a business on it. I've looked at desire from every angle and will probably continue doing so for the rest of my life. Because everything that's ever been manifested, created, made, or launched happened because of desire. It all starts there. And if you dig deep enough, I think that each of us will hit a bedrock of binary desires: to feel free and connected at the same time. Independent and Supported. Loved and Loving. Fluid and Rooted.

Deep positivity

Thought is pure energy. Every thought you have, have ever had, and ever will have is creative...All thoughts congeal; all thoughts meet other thoughts, crisscrossing in an incredible maze of energy, forming an ever-changing pattern of unspeakable beauty and unbelievable complexity.
– Neale Donald Walsch, *Conversations with God: An Uncommon Dialogue*

If there could be such a slogan for manifestation theory, this would be it:

Energy follows thought. Energy follows thought. Energy follows thought. And by the way...**energy follows thought.**

Manifestation happens from the mind.

For it to work effectively, you must achieve clarity of desire, root into the depths of positivity, fend off doubts with Faith, and repeat. Every minute of every day, give or take.

If you let your mind wander unattended into heavier thought-forms, like fear, or lack, or mistrust, then you'll likely hatch all sorts of chaos and attendant anxiety about that chaos. Notice I said "let your mind wander *unattended*." Because, inevitably, all kinds of negativity will cross your mind. If you're paying attention to that inner dialogue, you can redirect the conversation. If you train your mind to focus on "brighter" thought-forms (like courage, trust, kindness, abundance, one's right to joy), then you'll manifest more of those feelings, thoughts, and experiences.

Since **energy follows thought**, obviously, we want to keep our thinking—especially with respect to our creating our future—as "positive" as possible. But this is nowhere close to easy to do. It's intense work. Doubts will surface, mental garbage from our past will churn up, our daily life will still include bills to pay, relationships to nurture. Returning to positivity, consistently, can be the hardest thing *ever*. And the best. And the hardest. And the best.

Is staying consistently positive even possible? Yes. But it might not be what you think.

Let's break down "positive-think," because this is precisely where most manifestation techniques mess with our heads. Positive-think might suggest that it can make the bad things vanish. But "bad things" in life usually require some confrontation and management from our side. What's really problematic with positive-think is that we're being trained to use it *solely* to try to get what we want. This is shallow positivity. Stay with me. We need to be positive for multiple reasons: because it alleviates suffering, because it's good for our health, because it's a form of kindness.

If we're "thinking positive thoughts" just to manifest what's on our vision board, then what happens when we don't get what we want? We crash into negative thinking. Positive thinking has to be rooted in the heart, not in the attainment of stuff. We need to go much deeper.

> Deep positivity means that you have Faith that you'll be okay, *no matter what happens*. Not *if* it all works out for you in the end. Not *if* you get what you want when you think you should get it. No matter what.

Deep positivity knows that Life will have your back even when you don't manifest what you want.

Let your energy follow *that* thought.

We can also go wider with our definition of positivity. Negative emotion doesn't curse our creative efforts. Emotion is not the same as thought. Feeling angry isn't the same as thinking angry thoughts. You might feel mad about someone's actions—we'd likely label this a "negative" emotion. But you could think positively (or creatively) about it: "I'm glad that happened. Now I'm clear on the situation; I know what action to take." You can be enraged over a social injustice, and that rage will bring forth positive thinking in the form of solutions to the problem.

Soul reasons

In my experience, desire works best when you have intersecting reasons for wanting what you want. You want it for yourself, and you want it for others. You want it for pleasure, and to be of service. You want it because having it gives you joy, and you can send that joy (or money, or resources, or healing) out in other directions.

Desire has more potential to manifest when you intend to bring people up with you. There's nothing wrong with doing something for yourself, or just for someone else, but a steady diet of that leads to self-absorption or burnout. When our desires include others, we naturally open our hearts and minds, which only allows more good energy and thinking to flow into us. And I think Life is thrilled when our getting is braided with our giving. There's a very sacred efficiency to that and the Universe loves to support such elegant systems.

Certainty

Today I am handing the deep desire of my heart over to divine intelligence, in complete acceptance of its fulfillment. Gratefully, and with complete conviction, I am receiving this answer in my experience.

– Ernest Holmes, founder of Religious Science

Let's just assume that you're a manifesting powerhouse. You have the capacity to make dreams come true. You are the Queen of It's A Done Deal. That being the case, don't ask for something until you're really sure that you want it, because your wish is the Universe's command.

Think of it like this: you're putting in orders with the cosmic delivery service in the sky. Once you click "ORDER," your request gets forwarded to the creative department to be designed and manufactured, then to the pick 'n' pack department, then to shipping. Energy is already being expended on you. Your crew is on top of it.

And then…you change your mind and realize you don't actually want that order—that relationship you desired, that promotion you hoped for, that project you wanted to be involved with—and you cancel your "shipment." That's cool; you can cancel at any time. But your cosmic crew could have put that energy toward something that you were really certain about wanting—like something that benefits your health, or your community, or your greater creativity.

And yes, the Universe has an abundance of support energy to give you, but you're human and therefore you have expandable but limited capacity to conduct energy currents. Manifestation requires energy—on all of your levels. Brain power, night dream power, willpower, physical power. All of it. You get what you can handle.

So why not focus your manifestation energy on what matters the most to you? The fewer things you're focused on getting, the more energy you and the Universe have to put toward them. This means you can make fewer things happen, but much sooner. It doesn't mean you reduce the idealism of each wish. Wish big! Just wish toward a target. Hit that man-ifestation, and move on to the next desire.

Narrowing your focus doesn't mean that you lay your other dreams to rest. By practicing the art of building up your energy, you actually increase your chances of making them happen. Think of it as Manifestation Project Management. Focus for the win.

Manifesting is tricky when it involves other people (and it usually involves other people)

Pre-determinism is philosophical bullshit. You can't control much outside of yourself. And it doesn't matter if three psychics said that you and So 'n' So were going to hook up. You can't out-will someone else's free will. Because that Soulmate you have your eye on? They actually have their own life plans that may or may not include you. (I know, babe; their life would be SO much better if you were in it. Believe me, I know.) And that big gig you're gunning for? There's a cadre of players and circumstances involved—circumstances that are completely out of your control.

The problem with many prediction and manifestation techniques is that we easily forget that other humans are involved in our manifesting. As much as we'd LOVE to, we can't control other humans. Other humans = variables and complications and heaps of crazy, free will.

Self-care

Self-help and self-Love have everything to do with self-care. But in my back 'n' forth dance with striving and no-striving, while hustling hard to make things happen and trusting they would, sometimes I was too exhausted to receive what was coming my way.

I'd been doing everything I knew how to do in order to create a certain career opportunity. I was envisioning, trusting, and meeting the Universe halfway with great sweat and strategy. And I was wearing myself down. I thought, *Even if it happens, I might be too exhausted to rock it.* That snapped me out of my hyper-hustle mode.

Like most overachievers, I still have to create games for myself, like, "If you take two days off in a row, you'll actually be even more productive when you get back at it." Now, this is a proven fact and it works every time; a fresh mind is more productive. But I deserve downtime just because I want it—not because it's another means to achievement. The more I practice, the better I get at this. My heart rules my day planner.

But mind tricks to boost self-care might have to be your operating strategy for a while. *If I get a massage then I'm all relaxed and receptive to what the Universe wants to give me.* Take good care of yourself because you deserve it, AND so you're better able to receive the fruits of your labour. Pleasure makes you more receptive...to more pleasure.

Predicting the future

When clairvoyants offer predictions of timing, it's important to remember that astral time is not the same as Earth time. At best, timing forecasts are 50/50. Also, the channel(ler) affects the message. Every medium naturally puts their fingerprint on what they deliver to you. That can be good, bad, or neutral. It's just something to be aware of. As my kid said of one psychic's prediction for me: "I think she was having a bad day when she told you that." Good days and bad days affect great seers.

And things change—YOU change, from day to day. What you and your astrologer predict for you today could be right on target with the information currently available. But you could do something tomorrow that alters that course or creates a wrinkle in time.

You have multiple possible futures—each of which could be equally incredible. Imagine ten thousand Soulmates. Nine hundred once-in-a-lifetime opportunities. Three hundred and forty winning tickets. Infinite big breaks. Meditate on multiple pleasurable outcomes and you will loosen your grip on things being exactly how you think you need them to be.

Abundance!

> *This could be our revolution:*
> *to love what is plentiful*
> *as much as*
> *what's scarce.*
> - Alice Walker, "We Alone Can Devalue Gold"

Is there enough to go around? Abundance consciousness is one of the sexiest things about New Agers, isn't it?

Believing there's always enough—in fact, more than enough—is invigorating and empowering when it comes to manifesting for your own life. We also need to be sure it doesn't cause complacency when it comes to social inequalities and injustice. Because when self-helpers get preachy about how "You just have to want it bad enough!" I just think, *Noooo, not exactly, because we don't all have access to the same opportunities.* I do believe that there's enough to go around, but when it comes to Earth's resources, we have a bit of a hoarding issue. There is enough pie for everybody on the planet, but there are a lot of pigs eating too much pie.

True abundance mentality creates solutions for inequalities.

Passionately unattached

Not picking and choosing doesn't mean that you have to cultivate being detached. You can try that, sure. But then you find you're terribly attached to your non-attachment. Like you're proud of your humility.
– Alan Watts

Many spiritual teachings instruct us to detach from the outcomes we're seeking. But there's an important, sanity-saving distinction to make—the difference between detachment and non-attachment. It seems subtle, but there's a big difference.

Detachment is hard on your heart—and it creates blocks to what you want. Non-attachment, on the other hand, is nourishing, and it's also much easier to put into practice.

Detachment is rigid: a bit chilly, a tad cranky, like an uptight intellectual who's cut off from their heart. And here's the thing: detachment is often a coverup for fear of not getting what you want. Detachment defends itself against fear of being disappointed. No wonder it can be a bit bitchy.

Non-attachment allows you to want in a rational and Faith-fuelled way.

Non-attachment is open and spacious. It can hold your intense longing, and it can hold possibility. Non-attachment knows that some things take time, that you have to meet the Universe halfway, that free will is the guiding force, and that anything is possible.

As Michael Beckwith said to me: "Detached is 'I'm not playing anymore. I'm taking my ball and going home.' Whereas non-attached is 'I'm playing full-out, but I'm not attached to an outcome.'" Ya, THAT.

I'm a student scientist of desire. I've experimented with detachment. I tried the chilly side of Buddhism. I even tried cynicism for a minute. (That didn't go so well.) Desire fuels me, and non-attachment is the oxygen that fans my creative flames.

I've talked to hundreds and hundreds of people about what they want and how they're going after it. There's so much mystery left to explore, but I know this in my bones:

You've got to want what you want with all your heart. Not just half of your heart, not kinda, not only if there's proof, or if it's easy, or if the funding is there, or if the timing is perfect. Nuh-uh. No half-ass desire; you've got to put your full ass into it.

Don't apologize for the ferocity of your desire. Declare it. Ask for it. Pray for it. The energy of your desire increases its potentiality and magnetism. Your expectations affect your reality. Expect the best. Give it all you got, and then...let it go.

Desire. Let go. Expect. Trust.

All in, and unattached. It's the paradox of manifestation.

love the
Truth
into being

18
DEVOTION

I think you're up for it

Name your God

Listen to me
I am one of you
desirous broken open perpetual

Do this

1. Name your god, before the night comes.
2. Sing out the name of your God.

Sing now and sing loud, while you can recognize the
sound of your voice.

Then

3. Bring your holy mouth to Love and ask for what
you want.

She was born for that sound of yours.

Devotion. Like, real devotion.

DEVOTION TO TRUTH SEEKING goes something like this: you're going to risk being disliked (actually, it's not a risk, it's inevitable). At some point you will be very misunderstood—and you won't know how much that stings until it happens.

You're going to take a hit for the team. Because you're not learning lessons just for your own good. Healing for one is healing for many.

You will burn the plans that you thought were the answer to your profound longing. You will pray, on your knees, with the flavour of begging in your throat. You will have to ask for help—the vulnerable kind of asking when you're terrified that the answer could be *No*.

You will humbly make amends. You will let people go. You will build walls (because every kingdom has walls). There's a good chance that you'll be profoundly lonely. By necessity, you will become your own Lover. You will feel it all—all in one day.

You'll have to get up really early after staying up way too late. You'll learn to bend time, and subsist on your own confidence. You'll put in your own money. You're going to do the hard work that integrity calls for, like a grown-up. After a while, you might even amaze yourself by not resenting it.

You will pass through the eye of a needle, stripped, shed, pared down to the pure pith of your power. The few people who have seen you so naked will never speak of that beauty to anyone else.

You will transmute heart-ripping pain into evolutionary leaps. You will find comfort in the rhythm created by commitment, and you will come to adore the discipline of freely giving and receiving. You will become a testament to the force of tenderness.

You will say *Thank You*—for all of it. And then you and that devotion of yours will keep on going.

Karma in the bank

> *I wanted you to see what real courage is instead of getting*
> *the idea that courage is a man with a gun in his hand. It*
> *is when you know you're licked before you begin. But you*
> *begin anyway and see it through no matter what.*
> – Atticus Finch, in *To Kill a Mockingbird*

Question: Will you still do it if your dreams might not come true? If the payoff doesn't come in this lifetime? Would you still work to accrue beautiful karma and positive thought-forms?

"Sometimes, cause and effect are centuries apart," historian and activist Rebecca Solnit reminds us. Or lifetimes and dimensions apart. Many of us can grasp the concept of living responsibly in a way that considers the seven generations ahead of us. It's much harder to consider that the fruits of our spiritual devotion may not be harvested in this given life; instead, our purification and consciousness-raising efforts might be tabulated more...*ephemerally*. Our work may not create major breakthroughs for us as individuals this time around, but it's contributing to our Soul's evolution and the healing of the collective. It's a Universal law: we will cash in on our karma when the time is right.

So, who's in? If only you and your Soul know how hard you're working? Will you continue to re-train your mental chatter, strive to consume less plastic, donate some coin from every paycheque? Will you still get up at dawn to meditate and practice mantras? Will you work to generate metta and blessings for someone who may never forgive or understand you? Will you steady on with random acts of elegance and playfulness, ethics and eco-Love when the populace make it seem like a lost cause?

Will you still give it your all, not knowing if your Love will flow back to you as soon as you might wish?

Most importantly, resoundingly, monumentally...will you do it all for your own fulfillment? Not to improve your deficiencies, or for approval ratings, or to please the cosmic council.

Will you devote yourself to your joy and allow that to be your offering to the world?

I think you're strongly considering it.

Because you're here.

Because devotion is the bridge to your Soul.

The joy of the Truth about joy

> *If the Heavens ever did speak*
> *She is the last true mouthpiece*
> – Hozier, "Take Me to Church"

For about a decade, I've been asking a question of spiritually astute people, especially the ordained kind: **"What do you think our true nature is?"** One sage smiled, closed his eyes and deeply inhaled, as if his favourite memory of summer rain had just wafted into the room. "Our true nature? Ahhh..." he said. "Joy." Some teachers meandered through ancient mysticism to bring me to their answer. One rabbi told me the answer was unknowable. Guru Singh and I built an epic text chain, back and forthing about "Soul as the driving force, joy as the emotion..." This question is a magical doorway in my life.

What do *you* think our true nature is?

For the longest time, I thought that joy was, ultimately, our true nature, the centre of our centre. That assumption felt close, but not quite there. After much more making, meditating, struggling, succeeding, raging, chanting, sweetening, risking, respecting, humbling, healing, and inquiring, I believe this:

Joy is what happens when you make contact with your Soul.

When I meet my Soul—in a moment of reflection that brings a revelation, in the ecstatic passion of merging, in the simplest of intimacies with moonlight or strangers at the corner store—then I experience joy.

When I am being as me as I can possibly be, well, that's *euphoria*, no matter what my expression results in. When I see how the Cosmic Genius guides every single detail of my life to make up the Grand Scheme of it, I feel incredible *joy*—so much that it fills me up and I rationalize that I must be made of the stuff.

Your joy is where you locate your white hot Truth—your pure-burning is-ness, from where you have the creative power to turn thought into matter. You want to know who you are? Follow the joy, it's your Soul's reflection.

Joy is not the same as happiness. Happiness is like good weather. It's the billowy clouds floating in the sky. Joy is the atmosphere created by Truth, the whole sky itself, accommodating every experience from sunshine to tornadoes. Happiness comes and goes. Joy is ever present.

This is why, even in horrible sorrow, we can still feel the joy of being connected to our Truth. Joy is foundational; you can put anything on top of it. This means that it's possible to grieve intensely and still sense joy. You can feel bitter, and be aware of joy waiting patiently for your return. You can be hollowed out by loss, and feel held by the container of the joy of your existence.

Some people can be swimming in emotional shit and still declare, *I'm getting to the greater Truth—whatever it takes, however long it takes.* And with those friends, you should get in there and shovel, share in the weeping, climb, incant, and wait, actively, as long as it takes. Because they will teach you how to become really, truly joyful.

If you want to increase your joy, deepen your devotion to knowing the Truth. The Truth of who you are.

All on purpose

Do practice while you can. You'll need it when you can't.
– Krishna Das

When I travelled with friends to meet with the Dalai Lama in Dharamsala, India, we anticipated visiting a community steeped in tranquility and harmony. But the week before our arrival, there had been a horrible event in which three monks were murdered, most shockingly, by other monks. The story was on everyone's mind and in our meeting with His Holiness, the first thing we did was outpour our condolences. His response captivated me.

"Ah, yes, thank you for your thoughts," he said. "This is why we practice, for times like these when compassion is so necessary." He didn't engage our obvious disturbance about the event. He was soft and...very practical.

This is why we practice.

For times like these.

You don't need to be forgiving until you need to forgive. You don't need nerves of steel until your every last nerve has been taxed. You don't need to call on your Faith until you've spent all of your optimism.

This is why we practice.

This is why, even when life is ambling along quite nicely and our spiritual bank account feels flush, we still get ourselves to yoga, or to the support group, or to Sunday services.

When we feel safe, and aware of our privilege, we continue to question if there is more to reality. When we're high on hope, we keep asking for healing. And even though we could coast through society on our basic kindnesses, we keep standing up with disruptive definitions of progress and Love.

Because the day will most certainly come, whether you are a whole-hearted Light worker or in denial of grace, when you will be struck down by what life needs to show you. It can come in tiny, tearing heartbreaks during a walk through your neighbourhood. It can come in a tragedy, the likes of which could only happen once in a lifetime.

And when that time comes, you will need to withdraw the insights that you put into your heart's escrow. And you will need to call on your people—the unseen and the ones right in front of you—to help you meet the challenge.

You will be interrupted on your way to fulfillment. You will be asked who you are and why you are here. You will be called on to expand.

This is why we practice.

Go forth, from within

The best self-help is self-compassion. When you give yourself credit for making it this far in life—and still being a Gentle Soul—then you'll know the Truth of Love. When, in a courageously still moment you hear yourself say, "I have everything I need right now," then you'll know the Truth of Faith.

And you'll bring that shine to work with you. And to your causes, and your Loving, and your collaborations with the Universe.

You will not be fearless, but you will be certain of what matters most. You will place your preferences on the altar of your life and say: *This! THIS is what brings me joy.* And with the heavenly madness of Faith, you will live your Truth with the devotion it deserves.

May your beauty dawn on you.
May your pure Faith light the way.
May all be so blessed.

And hey...slow down if you need to, but don't ever stop.

THANK YOU

Having someone read what you write, to consider your words, to attend to each paragraph...it's an incredible interaction that I'll never take for granted. So Thank You for doing all you had to do to get these pages in your hands.

Chela Davison, Christina Platt, and Lianne Raymond volunteered to read the early drafts of this book and that gesture alone made me want to weep with gratitude. Every comment they offered felt like a gift with a bow on it. With elegance, Jennifer Gandin Le edited this book to make my philosophizing comprehensible and bring me up to date on political correctness. Siri Moyhan's wise questions made me think harder when I thought that I'd thought it all through.

Every Tuesday for many months, Steph Corker asked me, "So what do we need to do so you have more time to write?" And then she helped me do that. Candis Hoey did what she's been doing for years: kept me laughing and true to myself.

Many of my gritty and hilarious self-help lessons were experienced via my New Age Buddy system with Dr. Deb Kern—our laughs and tears are baked into these pages. Hiro Boga was a stream of clarity. Michael Barden, Terri Cole, Gabby Bernstein, Lisa Braun Dubbels, Anne Davin, Marie Forleo, Kate Northrup, Carrie-Anne Moss, Joshua Pettinato, Rochelle Schieck, Sam Reynolds & Pete McCormack, Linda Sivertsen, Danielle Vieth, Meggan Watterson, Mike Watts, and my mother Annabelle, have been beautiful nodes of Light, cheerleaders, reality checkers, late night tea makers, and the truest of friends. Nadia Prescher reminded me to do it my way. Guru Singh said what he saw. Lady Ninja of the Light showed me what devotion *really* means.

Nearly every month for seven years running, I've been meeting with Karis Hiebert, Dolly Hopkins, Michelle Pante, and Lee-Anne Ragan in our aptly named "Goddess Group." What we've been through together in that time could fill a whole book with gratitude.

I was hard to get a hold of while writing this book. I have Angie Wheeler and Victoriya Bobbitt to thank for that, and for at least fifty percent of all the great things in my life. They are the creative and strategic huge-hearted geniuses who take every idea I have and make it smarter and more beautiful. Our trifecta is one of the greatest blessings. Team D is a group of kind Souls who love to make things happen at the right time, from every time zone, with impeccability, and I want to do right by them for many years to come. Laurie Millotte designed this beautiful book-reading experience.

Heidi Krupp and her K2 team swooped in, like angels do, to carry us even higher. We are blessed.

For each person mentioned here, I place my hands on my heart and say 108 *Thank-You's*, smiling.

And to my son, HLJ: You are the whole, amazing, gorgeous, wildly creative reason why I tell the Truth. And I will spend every day of this and many lifetimes showing you how grateful I am for who you are. Thank you for making the burritos while I make the books. L-O-V-E.

INDEX

A

abundance consciousness, 217

acceptance, 8, 27. *See also* self-acceptance; tolerance

Active Child, 159

advice, 152

Affiliation, Lie of, 33–34. *See also* community

alternative medicine, 54

Amma (Karunamayi), 139–40

Angelou, Maya, 197

anger, 126

Anthony, Carol K., 191

antidepressants, 55

apathy, 126

apologies, 71

Archangel Michael, 190

ascension, *see* transcendence

asceticism, 90

astronauts, 51

Authority, Lie of, 30–32

awareness, 183

B

Bacon, Francis, 200

barriers, 105–6

bath recipe, 5

Beckwith, Michael Bernard, 79, 218

beliefs, changing, 41–42

bio healers, 54–56

blame, misplaced, 81

Blavatsky, H.P., 141

Boga, Hiro, 105

Bohr, Niels, 37

boundaries: advice to author's son, 103–4; around service, 128; vs. barriers, 105–6; common lack of, 9; difficulty accepting, 101; difficulty creating, 102, 104; healthy, 70; importance of, 101, 103, 105, 106–7; Lianne Raymond on, 104–5; practice needed for setting, 106

Bracco, Tara, 128

breatharians, 88

Brown, Brené, 66

Buber, Martin, 39

Buddha, 161–62

Buddhism, 8, 53, 56, 76, 89, 206. *See also* Dalai Lama

burnout, 127

C

D

K

Kali Yuga (age of vice), 148
karma, 52, 57, 147, 225
Karunamayi (Amma), 139–40
King, Martin Luther, Jr., 144–45
Kohut, Heinz, 99
Kornfield, Jack, 63, 111
Krishnamurti, Jiddu, 183, 199
Kundalini, 141, 171–72

L

liberation, 5–6, 27
lies: acceptance of, 24–25; of affiliation, 33–34; of authority, 30–32; Fantastically Flawed Premises, 26–27; of inadequacy, 27–30; power of, 24; role in seeking Truth, 23; spiritual economy dependent on, 25
life balance, 8
life coach, 31
Light: co-existence with dark, 124, 175, 190; mind as transmitter of, 40; seeking, 132
Light worker: as darkness peddlers, 144; and discernment, 188; mission of, 41; need for, 148; and resistance to forgiveness, 117; work aspect of, 172. *See also* gurus
loneliness, 70
Love, 68. *See also* self-Love

M

Mandela, Nelson, 203
manifestation: abundance consciousness, 217; deep positivity, 212–13; energy needed for, 214; involvement of other people, 215; management of, 214–15; paradox of, 219; and predicting the future, 216–17; problems with teachings on, 210; process of, 211–12; and self-care, 216. *See also* desire
mantras, 90, 170
manufactured consent, 125
Mary Magdalene, 162
Masters, Robert Augustus, 10, 192
materialism, 24, 210
media, 125–26
medication, 54–56
meditation, 170–72, 179–81
mental illness, 40
Merton, Thomas, 14, 88
Messiah Complex, 78
metaphysical analysis, 198–99
metaphysical technologies: approach to, 168, 176; crystals, 167, 174–75; Kundalini, 171–72; mantras, 170; meditation, 170–72, 179–81; mudras, 169; psychedelic drugs, 173–74; purification rituals, 173; vision boards, 172
Michael (Archangel), 190
mind, 40–41
miracles, 143

psychedelic drugs, 173–74
psychotherapy, 52–53, 56
psychotropic medication, 54–55
purification rituals, 173
puritanism, 44–45

Q
questioning, 8, 26, 38–39

R
Raymond, Lianne, 104–5
rebelliousness, 160
reincarnation, 200–201
relationships: avoiding toxic, 98; foolish compassion in, 102–3; and manifestation, 215; open, 157–58; for personal health, 69; as self-reflection, 100–101; tolerating problems in, 96–97. *See also* community; sexuality
righteousness, 25–26
risk taking, 70
rites of passage, 11–12
rituals, spiritual, 182
Rollins, Henry, 31
Ruiz, Don Miguel, 70
Rumi, 81

S
Sadhguru, 7, 170, 174
sādhus, 89–90
Salzburg, Sharon, 63
samsara, 8
Sathya Sai Baba, 136, 137–39
satori, 76
selectivity, 79
self-acceptance, 66–67, 68, 69-70, 82–83
self-care, 55–56, 68, 215–16, 229. *See also* boundaries
self-compassion, 202, 229. *See also* compassion
self-criticism, 7–8, 61–63. *See also* self-hatred
self-forgiveness, 118–19. *See also* forgiveness
self-hatred, 7, 61, 63–64, 65. *See also* self-criticism
self-help industry, 15. *See also* self-care
self-improvement, compulsion to, 7–8
self-loathing, *see* self-hatred
self-Love: difficulty achieving, 61, 64–65; expansion of Love to others, 71; faking it to achieve, 67; guarantee of, 72; other's reactions to, 72; self-acceptance as starting point, 66–67, 68, 70; self-hatred along path to, 65–66; signs of, 67–72
service: boundaries around, 128; burnout, 127; definition of, 126; importance of, 148; starting point, 128–29; suffering as, 206; using your body, 130; using your money, 130; using your soul, 130–31; using your voice, 129–30; for the wrong reasons, 127. *See also* practice

Tolle, Eckhart, 76, 80

Tolstoy, Leo, 33

transcendence: burning out on attaining, 90; experience with Dalai Lama, 140; experience with Karunamayi (Amma), 140; fascination with, 88; for laypeople, 89; super human path to, 91, 92; through asceticism, 89–90

transformation, 8

true nature, 226–27

Trungpa, Chögyam, 102

Truth: desire for, 39; flexible absolutism, 39–40; as journey, 6; messiness as inevitable, 44–45; mind as filter for, 40–41; purists seeking to protect, 44–45; spectrums of, 41; transmission of, 44

trying, rewards for, 69

Tyson, Neil deGrasse, 124

U

unbotherability, 79

V

validation, 31–32, 69, 82, 127

vipassana meditation, 90, 180

vision boards, 172

W

waking up, 126

Walker, Alice, 217

Walsch, Neale Donald, 211

Watts, Alan, 39, 80, 218

Welwood, John, 10

White, E.B., 124

Wiesel, Elie, 188, 204

Williamson, Marianne, 96, 129

wisdom: components of, 152; as paradoxical, 46; through personal attunement, 31, 150–51, 153

Woodman, Marion, 80

world, as mirror, 72, 100–101

Y

Yeats, W.B., 149

Yogi Bhajan, 141

Z

zealousness, 25–26

Zen Buddhism, 76. *See also* Buddhism

WHITE HOT TRUTH:
THE WORLD'S HOTTEST
BOOK CLUB

A guide for conversation & contemplation

The only thing more potentially life-enhancing than thinking about the meaning of life, is having a conversation about the meaning of life.

Call it a **book club**. Or church time. Or date night. Or go solo and make this an **ongoing journaling practice**. Do it over the course of a few weeks, or as the spirit moves you. You're already here, facing your heart—so why not take it deeper?

I'm offering a range of questions inspired by each chapter. Take what you want and leave the rest. And if you want to keep it simple, then you could use this set of questions as a reflection point for every single chapter theme:

What did you relate to? What do you see more clearly now? Does this change how you feel or what you'll do?

There is an even juicier extended **World's Hottest Book Club Guide for Conversation & Contemplation** at **DanielleLaPorte.com.** It's a free program, laid out in a calendar format with suggestions for group facilitation, more questions, and wrap-up exercises. Go get it.

If you want to share your Book Club experiences with us, please email **bookclub@daniellelaporte.com,** or use **#whitehottruth** on social media so we can find you.

Here's to clarity and keeping it real on your spiritual path.

Chapter 1 THE CHURCH OF SELF-IMPROVEMENT
When worship feels like work

- **What can you relate to** in Danielle's personal story of "sincere spiritual aspiration versus the compulsion to improve"?

- **Take an inventory of your self-help & wellness regime.** What are you doing that's really working for you? How do you know it's working? Which disciplines feel liberating, what feels like a chore? What practices do you need to retire?

- Regarding "motives" for spiritual growth... Where has there been **spiritual striving in your life?** Who are you trying to impress, or gain respect, or approval from? Does that feel negative or positive?

- When do you feel **spiritually "behind"** or "unevolved"?

Chapter 2 THE REALLY BIG LIES
The falsities we (inevitably, and necessarily) fall for on our way to Truth

- Re: **The concept of Original Sin.** Discuss. How does this concept show up in your life? How has it affected your sense of spirituality?

- Re: The Lie of Affiliation. **When have you fallen into groupthink?** When and how did you break away from it?

- When has belonging to a group been **truly comforting** and evolutionary for you?

- **Describe your current tribe.** Is it different than your tribe growing up? Is it what you want it to be?

Chapter 3 TRUTHFULLY SEEKING
How wisdom happens (hint: paradoxically)

- What's a metaphysical or spiritual concept that **you used to believe in?** What changed your mind about it? What do you believe now on that subject?

- Name two or three **contradictions about yourself.**

- Cite some examples of **spiritual hypocrisy.** Which of those do you have no patience for, and which can you accommodate?

Chapter 4 HEALING INSTINCTS
Mixing our own medicine (it's all an experiment)

- Who and what makes up **your "healing team"?**
- What are you **currently trying to heal**, and how are you doing that?

Chapter 5 FULL OF YOURSELF
The curiosities of self-hatred, and the only guarantee of self-Love

Talk or write about these self-Love topics:

- **Self-loathing.** Is it a natural human experience or just a curiosity of western culture?
- **Faking self-Love** to get more Love from others.
- **Befriending your loneliness** on your spiritual journey.
- **"Tolerating" your so-called shortcomings** vs. truly accepting them.
- **Holding out for the right thing** is not the same as passively waiting around for it.

Chapter 6 YOU'RE SPECIAL—BUT NOT *THAT* SPECIAL
In search of worth

- Have you ever used your **"spiritual" progress as posturing** to make you look better? When have you had the experience of someone's spiritual superiority creating separation between them and you?
- Is there a type of "spiritual" person that you **envy?**

Chapter 7 SUPER. HUMAN.
Choosing to really be here

- When do you feel **closest to God**, life, a higher power?
- When do you feel **the most human** and "earthly"?

Chapter 8 OPEN, GENTLE HEART. BIG FUCKING FENCE.
Boundaries for spiritual people

- Alright…let's go there. Talk about a time when you were **insanely loyal, foolishly compassionate, and/or excessively tolerant.**

- When have you considered that someone you were in a relationship with was **your emotional mirror?**

- Describe your understanding or experience of the difference between **boundaries vs. barriers.**

- What qualities does someone need to have to get through the **"big fucking fence that protects your open, gentle heart"?**

Chapter 9 READY TO FORGIVE
The complicated, gritty path to grace

- Have you ever **held back on forgiving**—and been comfortable doing so? What was that experience like?

- How has **forgiving someone shifted** your life?

- What's your experience of **forgiving yourself** and how did that shift things for you?

Chapter 10 THE SOUL OF SERVICE
Conscious optimism and giving from your fullness

- Do you think our **"enlightenment is inevitable"?** Do you believe that it's "all progress"?

- How do you deal with **feeling unable to help suffering people**—locally and globally?

- Is there a way in your life that you're **over-giving?**

- Where or how are you feeling **called to give more?**

Chapter 11 YOU ARE THE GURU
The hottest truth of all

- Have you been or **are you a devotee** of a spiritual teacher? Why them?

- Whose teachings and philosophies resonate with **you** most deeply?

- What's an idea or teaching that created **a paradigm shift** for you?

- Have you experienced **spiritual rapture via another person?**

- Have you experienced **the abuse of spiritual power?** How did the truth of that situation come to light?

- Have you had a **prodigal return** to any aspects of your original spiritual or religious upbringing?

Chapter 12 FAUX FREEDOMS
When sacred sex goes sideways

- So, like, what's **creeped you out** in the New Age "sexual liberation" scene?

- What has helped you **access and liberate** your sensual, sacred, and erotic power?

Chapter 13 POWER TOOLS
More awareness, deeper respect, less dependency

- Are there any spiritual "tools" that you've had a negative experience with? What spiritual gear have you let go of? What spiritual practices and/or tools are you curious to explore or integrate into your life?

Chapter 14 THE PATH WITHIN YOUR PATH
The roundabout journey to life-affirming discipline

- What's your relationship to meditation? Yoga? Clean eating?

- How have you taken traditional practices and made them your own? Where have you become more or less disciplined?

Chapter 15 DISCERNMENT IS EVERYTHING
When the negative serves the positive

- Has trying to **maintain spiritual harmony** ever kept you from calling bullshit?

- What New Age issues do you have strong opinions or discernments about that might be **easily labelled as "judgments"?** And how do you know when you're being discerning and not judgmental?

Chapter 16 REGARDING SUFFERING
Soul, pain, perspective

- Have you ever felt **"spiritual shame"** for your suffering or your personal development failures?
- In relation to your trials and tribulations, **what exactly are you grateful for?**
- What's your point of view on **why we attract** or create suffering in our lives? Do we choose it on a Soul level? Does the Creator dispense it to us for our growth or other reasons?
- How do you handle and respond to **other people's extreme suffering?** Is there anything you want to change about the way you typically respond?

Chapter 17 DESIRE, REFINED
A broader view for creating reality

- When have you actively tried to, and **successfully manifested**, something? Does that achievement influence how you're trying to manifest other things?
- Consider your current desires. Which ones are you *unattached* to—you really want it, yet you feel a sense of spaciousness around it? What are you acting *detached* from—you want it but you're not counting on it? And what are you definitely *over attached* to—you're going crazy with craving to have it?

Chapter 18 DEVOTION
I think you're up for it

- "Will you still do it if your dreams might not come true? **If the payoff doesn't come in this lifetime?** Would you still work to accrue beautiful karma and positive thought forms?" How does this question make you feel? Does it shift anything for you?
- What are you **devoted** to?
- If "the best self-help is self-compassion," how could you be more **compassionate with yourself**?
- What will you place on the metaphorical altar of your life to say: **"This! THIS is what brings me joy!"?**

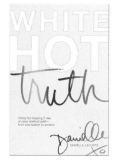

WHITE HOT TRUTH

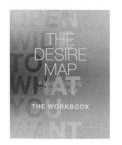
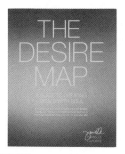

THE DESIRE MAP

YEARLY DAY PLANNER

THE FIRE STARTER SESSIONS

#TRUTHBOMB DECKS

ABOUT THE AUTHOR

Photo: Catherine Just

Danielle LaPorte is a member of Oprah's *SuperSoul 100*, a group who, in Oprah Winfrey's words, "is uniquely connecting the world together with a spiritual energy that matters."

She is author of ***White Hot Truth: Clarity for keeping it real on your spiritual path—from one seeker to another***, and ***The Desire Map: A guide to creating goals with soul***—the book that has been translated into 9 languages, evolved into a yearly day planner and journal system, a Top 10 iTunes app, and an international workshop program with licensed facilitators in 15+ countries. She is also the author of ***The Fire Starter Sessions: A guide to creating success on your own terms***, which also spun off into a workshop and coaching curriculum.

Named one of the "Top 100 Websites for Women" by *Forbes*, millions of visitors go to **DanielleLaPorte.com** every month for her daily #Truthbombs and what's been called "the best place online for kickass spirituality."

A former think-tank exec, now a speaker and poet, Danielle's charities of choice are VDay: a global movement to end violence against women and girls, and charity: water, setting out to bring safe drinking water to everyone in the world.

She lives in Vancouver, BC with her favourite philosopher, her son. You can find her **@daniellelaporte** and just about everywhere on social media.